Changing Family Lifestyles

Their Effect on Children

James D. Quisenberry, Coordinating Editor
Lucy Prete Martin, Editor
Mary N.S.W. Parker, Editorial Assistant
for Special Publications

CONTENTS

Editor's note: These articles are reprinted from CHILDHOOD EDUCATION. To minimize production costs, we have not attempted to update the material, including authors' professional affiliations.

Association for Childhood Education International
3615 Wisconsin Avenue, N.W., Washington, D.C. 20016

Foreword

IN ORDER to provide the field with a collection of useful information on a topic crucial both to children and those who care about them, the ACEI Publications Committee has planned this bulletin dealing with aspects of the family and family life. In surveying sources, we were happy to find that many facets of this topic have been addressed in thoughtful and thought-provoking articles in CHILDHOOD EDUCATION — more, in fact, than were needed to fill these pages.

In this collection of articles you will find a variety of basic family problems dealt with from several points of view — black and brown as well as white, male as well as female, parent as well as teacher, early adolescence as well as early childhood. Much that is good in our family systems is also included to help keep the problems in balanced perspective. Some of the articles address the professional community, some the lay public. For further study, several of the articles include references and sources representing basic, current research and theory (about 60 references in all). In short, this is a "state of the art" publication on the family.

We hope that your particular interest is addressed in this bulletin. Through it, the strengths existing in our family systems may be enhanced to some degree and the problems facing them come nearer to needed solutions.

James D. Quisenberry, Coordinating Editor
and Incoming Chairperson, ACEI Publications Committee
Curriculum, Instruction and Media Department
Southern Illinois University, Carbondale

Family Folklore

Amy J. Kotkin and Holly C. Baker

WHEN DID your family come to the United States? Do you know any stories about how they got here and where they first settled? Do your parents tell any stories about their childhoods? How does your family celebrate birthdays? Did your parents ever make up bedtime stories for you? Are there any photograph albums in your family? Do you take home movies?

For the past three summers, members of the Family Folklore Program have been asking these and related questions of visitors to the Smithsonian Institution's annual Festival of American Folklife. While the Festival as a whole features traditional folk performers from regional, racial and ethnic groups in the United States and from abroad, the Family Folklore Program focuses on the festival visitors. The Program fosters the realization that, as part of a family, each festival-goer is part of a folk culture all his or her own.

FAMILY FOLKLORE
AT THE FESTIVAL

Family Folklore was founded in 1974 to give festival visitors an unusual perspective on folk culture by encouraging them to recognize that their own lives are filled with folklore. Following the general festival policy of providing both entertainment and education, Family Folklore attempts to demonstrate to the public that the stories, expressions and traditions so common in their own lives are forms of folklore just as creative, artistic and valid as those performed on the festival stages. We hope our informants will begin to understand that folklore is not an item that can be performed on a stage or an artifact that can be displayed in a museum case, but a living, ongoing process that is part of everyone's life. By showing how folkloric elements function as

special yet everyday parts of the lives of our informants, we hope to lead visitors to a better understanding of the function of folklore in the lives of festival performers. The extraordinary fiddling featured on the festival's main stage may be to the fiddler just a way to pass a Saturday night back home. Conversely, the story of a grandfather's journey to the United States, which has become routine to his family from frequent retelling, may be full of melodramatic appeal to a new listener. We ask our informants to step back and see their own traditions in the same light as they see the traditions framed on a stage and labeled as folklore.

Rather than observing the skills and talents of others, visitors to our area become performers themselves. Every person who comes into our tent is invited to be interviewed on tape about the stories and traditions that are part of his or her family. Festivalgoers are asked to recount stories about events that took place generations ago or as recently as yesterday. Other topics range from ways of celebrating holidays to games played in the family car. What we try to do is to make people aware of the traditions that are part of their lives and of the value and beauty of those traditions.

All of us who have worked in the Program can remember the few days before our exhibit opened in 1974. The idea that every family has its own folklore, that creative, artistic expression is part of all our lives, was fine in theory. But would visitors sacrifice watching a musical performance or craft demonstration to perform their own stories

and traditions, to share their own folklore with us? Much to our delight, they proved eager and willing to tell their stories. The success of that first summer indicated that we had tapped an important resource in the American consciousness. With that base, we expanded and clarified our understanding of family folklore.

Functions

From our perspective, family folklore serves several functions. *First,* it enables individuals to place themselves in their family's structure and history. The "I" becomes at once granddaughter, daughter, niece, aunt, sister, cousin, mother, grandmother. Each relationship is reflected and reinforced by the folklore that is part of it. *Second,* family folklore enables individuals to place themselves in an historical context. How did their families fit into the tides of immigration? The settling of the West? The Depression? The larger panorama of American life? *Finally,* family folklore serves to bind families together. As one informant put it, "Family folklore is a kind of glue."

In our experience, visitors have often returned to tell us that our questions have rekindled material in their own family. It is not uncommon for people to return several times with different members of the family or with new stories they have learned. Referring to storytelling situations in his own family, the same informant told us, "I think it's an attempt to dust off the cobwebs on memories that were pleasant. . . . It isn't a particular story or a particular event so much as an attempt to get everybody back on the same wavelength."

Amy J. Kotkin (on left, shown interviewing a festival-goer) and Holly Cutting-Baker, besides serving as active members of the Smithsonian Family Folklore Program, are both Ph.D. candidates at the University of Pennsylvania in Philadelphia.

Forms

Our interviews with over three thousand informants have enabled us not only to theorize about the functions of family folklore but also to broaden our understanding of the *forms* of family folklore. Perhaps the best example of this is the role of photography and home movies in family life. One day at the 1974 Festival, when we were still concentrating on recording oral traditions, a young woman whom we had interviewed on a previous day returned to our exhibit with a photograph album. The book was a wedding present from her mother in which the latter had traced four generations of the family through photographs. Until then we had regarded photographs simply as illustrations of family life. But Nancy Smith's album was not just an illustration; it was an integral part of her folklore. When we interviewed her again, we discovered a strong relationship between her photos and her stories. A picture of her great-aunt called forth the story of that aunt's dramatic escape from Russia in the early 1900s; a photo of Nancy's first car brought forth reminiscences of her teenage years. We began to see that photographs are the visual counterparts of stories and other verbal genres of family folklore. Whereas family stories are one way in which families "image" themselves verbally, family photographs represent the way this is done visually; the home photographer becomes the counterpart of the family story-teller.

In the next year and a half, over one hundred families shared their albums, slides and home movies with us. In the process of viewing them and talking with their owners, we became more fully aware of the ways such visual materials give family members an enhanced sense of roots and belonging as well as growth and change. The 1975 and 1976 programs were expanded accordingly. Home movies and family photograph albums were examined as important areas of creative expression and formed the major displays of the Family Folklore area. Ranging from blown-up reproductions of individual photo albums to panels chronicling the American life cycle in photographs, these displays of home photography have had a dual appeal to festival-goers. Not only have they proven visually stimulating and thought provoking in their own right, but they also have enabled families to see their own photographs as part of a larger visual tradition.

Home movies were compiled into a documentary film depicting them as a modern folk art. Central to the film was the concept that home movies are a good index to American ideals and values. As such, home movies are not an objective, random glimpse into our past, but an idealization of how we choose to preserve and present, to remember and be remembered.

The Family Folklore Program is constantly becoming aware of more and more ways by which families preserve their pasts. Continuing contact with our Festival informants has given us a glimpse into other methods utilized by families and individuals within families to record their history. Family history quilts, letters, diaries, memoirs, and memorabilia have joined stories and photographs in our displays of family folklore.

FAMILY FOLKLORE
GOES TO SCHOOL

Our experiences with the Family Folklore Program, specifically designed to function in a festival context, suggest that certain aspects of the Program can easily and effectively be adapted for use in an elementary school curriculum. Although most of our informants have been adults, we have interviewed many children. An example of a child's contribution is the following story told to us by an eleven-year-old:

> My great-grandfather had come from Poland, or right near Poland, and he came to this country during the Spanish American War. There was one of those Uncle Sam posters saying "Uncle Sam wants you" and he thought it meant him and he went and joined the Army. "Uncle Sam wants you," he wondered. "Me? Why me? What's so special about me, I just came to America."

The children we have interviewed have had two common characteristics. They have been interested in their families' histories and they have been receptive to learning

All photographs in this article are by courtesy of the authors with permission of the Smithsonian Institution, Washington, D.C. Above: some of the thousands of festival-goers who perused the albums, photo montages and other memorabilia at the Festival of American Folklore. Pages 3, 7, 8, some of the "treasures" of the Family Folklore Program archives. Schools can readily mount similar displays.

those histories. Family folklore is not synonymous with genealogy. There is no need to memorize names and dates and lines of descent—certainly dry fare for a child. Family folklore is learned by living as a member of a family, by listening to relatives talk about the family, by asking questions about the past. The material we have collected at Family Folklore has as much humor, drama and excitement as any piece of literature and, for children, the added appeal of belonging to *their* family. We believe that by the time they reach school age many children are already carriers of family folklore and are eager to share that folklore with others.

Many Benefits

Educators are in a superb position to utilize this resource, not only for its inherent interest but also for its possible applications within the classroom. At the very least, the study of family folklore adds a different dimension to units on the family. It can also enliven other subjects. For example, family folklore can make history more real by placing a child's own relative in historical context—what grandfather did in World War I, how great-grandmother crossed the country in a covered wagon. In social science, family folklore can help children understand and appreciate cultural differences and similarities by using family traditions of the students themselves as examples. The classroom use of family folklore would also be an excellent way to integrate home and school experiences. Benefits to the family itself would be increased interaction between generations as children ask about their families and greater appreciation of relatives by children.

Methodologies

For classroom use, family folklore can be collected directly from the children or the children can be encouraged to collect from their relatives. The first approach would be of use primarily to someone interested in collecting and studying the traditions carried by children, although it would certainly yield a fascinating body of material. On the other hand, having children do research themselves among their family members would yield far more material and, at the same time, provide the children with other benefits such as research skills and contact with relatives.

The methodology, whether used by teacher or student, can be very simple. All that is necessary are a list of questions, a means of recording answers (a tape recorder is ideal), enthusiasm and perseverance. Most questions can be very general, such as asking for stories about grandparents. Others can be designed to complement lesson units in other subjects; topics might be immigration (his-

tory), names (language), and occupations (social studies). Family folklore can also be related to the calendar year by asking about holiday traditions at appropriate times. Of course, questions can also be designed specifically to relate to the experiences of a given class, especially if it is composed predominately of students from similar backgrounds.

Photographs brought into class by students are an important supplement. Not only do they add interest to stories by providing faces for names and act as cues for remembering additional details or other stories, but they also serve to illustrate technological advances, changing styles, and historical events.

In Sum

The Family Folklore Program has a rich archive of family traditions and photographs built up over three years of interviewing within a festival context. Our research based on this material is only now beginning. The experience itself of collecting is so rewarding, both personally and academically, that we are trying to encourage others to expand our concepts and to work in fields beyond our reach. We hope we have succeeded.

For further reading:
Family Folklore Program, Smithsonian Institution. *Family Folklore.* Washington, DC, 1976.
———. *I'd Like To Think They Were Pirates.* Washington, DC, 1975.

The Changing Family and Early Childhood Education

Paz I. Bartolome

A GREAT DEAL is being said these days about the school's failure to develop among children the attitudes, knowledge and skills that will enable them to cope with their world and with themselves. The school is being blamed not only for the incompetencies of youth but for much of societal malaise. Bronfenbrenner, for instance, declares that "Schools have become potent breeding grounds of alienation in American society" (1973, p. 13).

This sentiment is influenced by the equation of schooling with education. In the past century schools have been given much of the credit for the accomplishment of the young. Historically, the educational contributions of other institutions, particularly the family, have been ignored. It is no wonder that the public holds the school completely accountable when children turn out to be poorly educated.

The Need for a Comprehensive Perspective

This lack of comprehensive perspective in education prevents educators and policymakers from asking the right questions and dealing with the right issues when they try to design and implement effective educational policies and programs for young children. Policies and designs are frequently developed based on the notion that education happens primarily in school settings. For instance, there is important evidence that in the earliest years children are more influenced by family than by peers or anyone outside the family, and that early intervention with children is most effective when it involves the parents and the home (Bronfenbrenner, 1974). Instead of taking advantage of the influence of the parents and the family in the schools, some early intervention programs do the opposite by involving trainers in clients'

homes teaching grandparents, mothers and fathers how to behave like schoolteachers!

In one report slides were shown of a trainer demonstrating to a grandmother how to use cutout construction paper to teach her grandchildren colors and shapes. Another report showed slides of a trainer with a mother who is hanging clothes in the yard with her child. The trainer is using a flannel board with cutout laminated pictures. In another instance, the trainer is showing both the father and the mother how to use cardboard puzzles with their children.

Who needs all these cutout construction papers and laminated pictures when the home is full of rich, meaningful and functional activities and materials for learning? These misguided and wasteful early intervention efforts assume that learning and instruction are products of the school alone: for learning to occur, parents should act like schoolteachers and things found in the schools should be brought into the homes. While we recognize the importance of the family, we still look at the schools as models for educational program designs and implementations.

This assumption is evident when educators suggest the need for public developmental child care centers and free public nursery schools for all 4-year-olds to counter the negative effects of poverty and the changing family. In terms of fulfilling the varying child care needs of working parents, planners and decision-makers in the field of education largely ignore the educational services provided by family child care homes. The potentials and possibilities of family settings as effective educational resources are ignored. Hughes (1976) points out that

... in emphasizing the importance of education, we have indirectly conveyed the notion that school-

9

A thought-provoking article, certain to involve readers in the content! The author stresses the need for a wider perspective of the family in designing policies and programs for children. Paz Bartolome is a Professor in the School of Education, University of North Carolina at Wilmington.

ing . . . is education and that all education therefore takes place at school (p. 24).

Caring for children in the home is seen as a custodial and babysitting service. There is little or no recognition that everyday activities in the home are excellent vehicles for learning and that home-based caregivers are effective educational and socialization agents.

Because of the narrow perspective in education, the bulk of research over the past 15 years has not provided educators and policymakers with much help in designing and implementing early education programs. A great deal of the so-called preventive and innovative programs have not answered the right questions, nor have they addressed the right issues. Since we are dealing with problems caused in part by family changes, policymakers and educators might wisely look back to examine what the family has done in the past and note what changes have taken place in family structures and functions. In so doing, they might gain some insights in designing and implementing effective policies and programs for young children.

The Family—Then and Now

In the past the family functioned as an economic unit. Most education took place at home, organized around maintaining the home and earning a means of livelihood. The family was responsible for helping children acquire many complex learnings including language skills and high-level psychomotor skills, as well as an almost infinite number of work-related values and attitudes. These skills, values and attitudes were not taught and learned as ends in themselves; they were taught and learned while the children were involved in meaningful and productive tasks. Children and parents con-

stantly interacted with each other while they worked to maintain and support the family. Generally speaking, the children were needed and, in being needed, had the chance and responsibility to make real contributions to the welfare of others. This in turn gave them feelings of dignity and personal worth. However wanting or deprived their lot may have been, the children felt useful and needed.

Industrialization and its accompanying educational upgrading and population concentration have changed the economic functions of the family. The family no longer operates as an economic unit: young children no longer participate in their parents' work; their years of dependency are lengthened. They are increasingly being segregated from the routine experiences of the adults in their lives.

Urie Bronfenbrenner (1973) points out that:

One of the most significant effects of age segregation in our society has been the isolation of children from the world of work. In the past, children not only saw what their parents did for a living, but even shared substantially in the tasks.

Nowadays, many children have only vague notions of the nature of the parent's job and have had little or no opportunity to observe the parent, or for that matter any other adult, when he is fully engaged in his work (p. 10).

In our effort to protect children from unfair labor practices, we have made them useless—a state that may have worse consequences than child labor. They have become consumers of society's wares and objects of affection who do not share in society's creative efforts and productive activities. No longer the economic blessings they used to be, children have become tremendous liabilities. What purpose is served when they are given meaningless "busy" work—projects we lavishly praise but do not use at home or school? How do the children feel when they see their creations in the trash can?

If children are to become responsible members of society, they must not only be exposed to adults involved in meaningful and demanding tasks, but they must themselves begin to participate in such activities early in life. We need to involve children in undertaking genuine responsibilities that will give them a sense of purpose, dignity and worth. Perhaps we can learn something from the Amish people, who involve their young children in the productive endeavors of the family.

In the past the family functioned as an intimate part of the community. Children intermingled with community members from different walks of life. These were people who cared, who shared parenting responsibilities and lent moral and social support to the children's families. Business offices and other community institutions were accessible places for children to observe adults work and interact socially. As a result, children had varying degrees of attachment to a diversity of adults who as role models helped them develop their self-concept and provided them with alternatives for their decisions and actions.

Today, as parents seek better job opportunities, families have become isolated from the world of work, from the community, and from relatives and friends. Homes have become private places where working members renew themselves for the next day's struggles in the world of work.

Zoning laws that emphasize space and privacy have shriveled the neighborhood experiences available to children. Parenting is no longer a shared responsibility. If family relationships become tenuous, no one intercedes except for an emergency situation (usually a policeman or a social worker). In spite of the changing structure of the family and the changing needs of the time, the myth that raising a family is the sole responsibility of individual parents is perpetuated. Consequently, young parents receive less support for parenting and growing children

receive less affection and guidance and less opportunity for socialization. As Kenneth Keniston (1977) points out:

The myth of self-sufficiency blinds us to the workings of other forces in family life. For families are not now, nor were they ever, the self-sufficient building blocks of society exclusively responsible, praiseworthy, and blamable for their own destiny. They were deeply influenced by broad social and economic forces over which they have little control (p. 12).

Some Alternatives in Designing Policies and Programs

To counteract the negative effects of family isolation, we must temper our ideas of individualism and privacy with a sense of community. We must make it possible for children to experience the environment as a series of interrelated institutions that appreciate children's existence and their potential contributions. The school, the parents' places of work and community institutions should be used as extensions of the family setting, complementing the role and function of the home. As their contribution to the education of the young, business organizations should allow parents to participate in school programs during working hours and welcome and encourage involvement of young children in their plants and business offices.

If we change our narrow perspective of education, we can focus attention on young children, their families and their relationships. We can then create ecological programs for the young, using the wealth of untapped resources available in the community to support and strengthen parents and teachers in nurturing, stimulating and caring for young children (Bronfenbrenner, 1977). Parents and teachers shoulder tremendous responsibilities for children's development—in isolation, while untold numbers of community members (particularly the young and the elderly) are seeking meaning in their lives. It is possible to create small educational settings, where people who know one another and who represent different occupations and walks of life intermingle with young children.

If we change our narrow perspective of the

(Clockwise)
Children become involved in a meaningful activity like gardening. They plant seeds, watch them grow and bear fruit.
Children visit a garden shop where they become involved with a real worker doing her job.
Children plant real seeds for the garden, which will not be discarded once they have sprouted.

Photographs courtesy of author

family, we can design and implement policies and programs that work for young children. Our cosmetic and fragmented approach toward educational research and development might be replaced by an ecological and wider perspective, making the results of our efforts to change and innovate more effective and lasting. Take, for example, the growing need for different types of child care services, the declining elementary school enrollment, and the growing alienation between the old and the young. In developing policies and programs, we would do well to seek answers to the following questions:

How can we recapture the feeling of importance and worth growing children used to have when the family functioned as an economic unit?

How can we re-create the community where parenting is shared and the community serves as an educational park for all children?

How can we reintroduce in the lives of children varying degrees of relationships with people from all walks of life who can serve as their models and influence future decisions and actions?

In the process of seeking viable answers to these questions, we might moderate our pre-occupation with the three Rs and with mechanical theories of hierarchical learnings and stages of development. We might develop learning centers where children are involved in useful tasks, where they can learn through concrete experiences while helping and watching adults from different walks of life perform their chores as contributing members of society. Such real-life experiences can contribute more to the over-all development of children than their present isolation in schools full of cognitively stimulating books and toys. As Bronfenbrenner points out (Brandt, 1979):

One of the most important things is to recognize that the school cannot work in isolation. School people must build bridges to the rest of the community and to the parents. They must create situations in which more of the community is in the lives of kids in schools, and the kids are more a part of the community. Now, some might say, "If kids spend their time in community activities, how are they going to learn to read?" My answer is, "Until they do that, they will not learn to read." Children learn to read not because there is some new gimmick to teach them, but because learning to read is considered an important thing. We saw that in China. They have the deadliest curriculum and the worst teaching methods you can imagine, but we couldn't find one child who didn't know how to read. The reason was that the classrooms were filled with people, old and young, who kept saying, "Reading is important; come read with me" (p. 463).

Basic academic skills can be acquired by children through meaningful and useful activities—not as ends but as means of living the good life. For instance, children can participate in early childhood activities like gardening, cooking and role-playing not merely to learn colors, numbers, shapes and sizes but to learn to support themselves, to share with others the fruits of their efforts, and to become effective members of their communities.

The study of community helpers need not be limited to discussions of pictures and listening to stories. It can include visiting *real* work places in the community and getting involved with *real* workers doing their tasks. In so doing, education is extended far beyond acquisition of reading, writing and ciphering skills to acquisition of such important life skills as problem-solving and decision-making.

Policy- and decision-makers should consider other alternatives to learning centers that may strengthen family ties and community involvement with young children. Whatever type of school arrangement is provided, the total community should be involved: school organizations, departments of social services, business organizations, labor unions and other groups active in the community. Children are our most valuable asset. It is high time we put our acts together, not only for their welfare but ours as well.

References

Brandt, Ron. "On Families and School: A Conversation with Urie Bronfenbrenner." *Educational Leadership* 36, 7 (Apr. 1979). Reprinted with permission.
Bronfenbrenner, Urie. "The Roots of Alienation." *Journal of the National Association for Women Deans, Administrators, and Counselors* (Fall 1973). Reprinted with permission.
———. *A Report on Longitudinal Evaluations of Preschool Programs.* Washington, DC: U.S. Department of Health, Education, and Welfare, 1974.
———. "Toward an Experimental Ecology of Human Development." *American Psychologist* 32 (July 1977): 513–31.
Hughes, Jerome M. "The Home as an Academy for Learning." *Elementary School Principal* 55, 6 (July/Aug., 1976).
Keniston, Kenneth, and the Carnegie Council on Children. *All Our Children.* New York: Harcourt, Brace Jovanovich, 1977. Reprinted with permission.

Editor's note: For a description of six successful parent education programs, see *Parent Education: The Contributions of Ira J. Gordon,* by Patricia Olmsted, Roberta Rubin, Joan True and Dennis Revicki (Washington, DC: ACEI, 1980). See also:

Frost, Joe L., et al. *Developing Programs for Infants and Toddlers.* Washington, DC: ACEI, 1977.
Schwartz, Judy I. "The Care of Infants and Toddlers in Group Settings." *Childhood Education* 56, 2 (Nov/Dec. 1979): 88-95.

Support Systems for Black Families

Joseph H. Stevens, Jr.

REARING socially and intellectually competent children is no simple task. It requires a great deal of support. And black families, like any other families, benefit from support in childrearing. This support and help may be forthcoming from informal sources like a parent network of close friends and relatives. It may also come from formal systems made up of professionals in institutions like the school, the church or the mental health center.

We have been preoccupied with constructing and designing formal support systems like parent education programs, Home Start programs and parent-child center programs that will enable parents to rear competent children. This is an important laudable goal. But we have worked toward it from ignorance. This is especially true in programs designed for the black community, for we have not attempted to uncover existing informal structures that enable black parents to rear children competently.

Fortunately, several forces have checked this missionary zeal. Foremost is a rise in black consciousness and pride which has demanded affirmation, not simply acknowledgment, of diversity in childrearing goals, outcomes and procedures. Second, we in the United States face a severely limited national economy no longer able to finance universal, omnibus "intervention" programs.

The third involves the scientific community. More than ever before we realize that what transpires between parent and child is profoundly influenced by (and influences) institutions and people outside the home: friends and family, community agencies and services, government programs and policies, cultural values and mores. To understand children's development we need to examine it in its broadest context—utilizing an ecological perspective (Bronfenbrenner, 1979). Fourth, we now see the need for examining systematically how government policy constrains or facilitates family functioning by using procedures like family impact analysis (Johnson and Ooms, 1980).

These forces have directed responsible human service providers and researchers to look for those natural supports available to families before programs are designed. Unfortunately, we as yet have little trustworthy data about these natural support systems and their effectiveness which we can use to guide us in program development. So the purpose of this paper must be to raise issues and indicate what type of additional information is needed.

Some social scientists have argued that the parent-child unit is too narrow a conceptualization of black family life. Gutmann (1976) found the black parent-child unit was enmeshed in a supportive social network, primarily composed of kin, even as early as the 1850s. And the majority of black families still appear to be intact (Sowell 1978).

McAdoo (1978) has argued that black families manifest a neo-local extended family structure (not a nuclear one), in which close linkages are maintained between several households of related individuals. Thus, the single-parent family and the nuclear family are surrounded by a close network of relatives and friends who pass for relatives. These linkages are based on the exchange of

Joseph H. Stevens, Jr., makes a strong case for not disrupting the "natural" childrearing support systems used by black families, systems that involve "the extended family and circle of kin and friends." The author is a Professor in the Department of Early Childhood Education, Georgia State University, Atlanta.

both emergency and everyday help, including help in childrearing. This appears to be one of the strengths of black families (Hill, 1972).

THE SOCIAL NETWORK: A NATURAL SUPPORT SYSTEM

McAdoo's extensive study (1978) of middle income black women revealed that the kin help system was widely utilized. However, single women interacted with and depended on relatives (and close friends) for help more often than did married women. Everyday child care arrangements were made generally with non-family; however, emergency and occasional child care was an important help provided by the social network of kin and friends. More help was forthcoming from family than from friends, though most women had networks containing both. Single women gave and received more financial help, whereas marrieds exchanged more emotional support.

Upward mobility of these black women was also related to help from others. Mothers who had moved from a working class background into a middle class adulthood had received more financial help from family, whereas those who were born into middle class families reported they tended to receive emotional support more so than financial support. Thus, help from family (especially financial assistance) may enable individuals to move to economically more secure situations.

Corroborative evidence is available that network support may help ensure that the parent is better able to care for the child. Furstenberg's study of black teenage mothers (1976) provides strong evidence that those who have support of a working spouse or of their own parents are economically better off later. And single teenage mothers who continue to live with their parents are more likely to complete their schooling and move from welfare to economic independence.

These types of exchange systems and network relationships may not always benefit the parent or the child. Stack (1974) has suggested that strong reciprocal ties around the exchange of money may work to keep low-income mothers in poverty. When all network members have quite limited resources, no one member can afford not to request fairly quick return of money provided on loan. Thus, the sharing of quite limited resources may enable all network members to survive, but may not make upward mobility possible. In contrast, where one's budget is less tight, a friend or relative might be willing to accept help or emotional support as an immediate repayment and defer in-kind repayment until later.

One can quickly extrapolate about the possible ripple effects throughout a particular network, where one individual obtains a better paying job through fair employment laws. To affirm the face validity of this concept of the economic interdependence of the black extended family, simply recall "A Raisin in the Sun" and the potentially divisive struggles about whether the father's insurance money should be used to buy the mother's dream home (thus preserving the family's integrity) or to enable the son to start a business (thus ensuring the family's economic future).

THE BLACK SOCIAL NETWORK
AND CHILDREARING

The black parent's social network of friends and family seems to play a significant role in the rearing of children, irrespective of socioeconomic class. Stack (1974) observed how members of a parent network actively participated in the care and disciplining of children.

> The exchange of children and short-term fosterage, are common among female friends. Child care arrangements among friends imply both rights and duties. Close friends frequently discipline each other's children verbally and physically in front of each other (p. 82).

Childrearing among these women was not viewed as the total responsibility of the mother, but as a task to be shared—one in which network members might be expected to share. In this setting, it is easy to see how the mother's friends and relatives might sanction her parenting behaviors, provide alternative models for both the child and the mother, and share specific information and values about childrearing. And these direct influences of the mother's social network on her behavior (through modeling, sanctioning, information transmittal) may well have important consequences for her parenting skill.

In my own study of some 300 low-income black families in a large southern metropolitan area, teenage mothers were found to be slightly less emotionally and verbally responsive than a group of adult parents who also had toddlers. However, some teenagers were just as positive in their responsiveness to their young children as were the adult mothers. When we examined a smaller group of teenage mothers who shared a significant portion of the rearing of their infants with their own mothers, we found the teen mothers were also less responsive and more punitive than were the grandmothers. These older black women may have been more responsive because of their greater maturity, experience in childrearing, and interest in and commitment to mothering. They probably function as potent models for such behavior—at least for some teenage mothers.

We also examined whether a number of aspects of the mother's behavior and characteristics of her network were correlated with her infant's development. We did find significant multiple correlations which are reported more extensively elsewhere (Stevens, 1980). We found that mothers who were more emotionally and verbally responsive and who had networks composed of more females had toddlers who were developing better, as measured by the Bayley Scales of Infant Development. We might infer that more female network members enabled toddlers to develop better because there were more caregivers available to stimulate and care for them. Informal observations support this to some extent; it was not uncommon for these toddlers to visit with the teenage mother's own mother, aunt, sister or girlfriend. These visits occurred in some cases with regularity and might last a few days.

A second relationship is possible. Young infants who are already developing better might attract the attention of skillful women interested in children and their care. Thus, alert, attractive, responsive, sociable, flexible and bright black infants may be borrowed for overnight visits; taken on walks in the neighborhood and to the store; presented with gifts of toys, diapers or clothes; and played with more often. Thus, the infant may influence the composition of his or her mother's social network and enable her to establish and maintain relationships with certain types of individuals.

These are important hypothetical transactions in development that only longitudinal research can clarify. Yet they illustrate how we need to press onward to gather information about the natural supports available to black parents.

HELP FROM SOCIETALLY CONSTRUCTED SUPPORT SYSTEMS

Various community institutions and agencies provide services and programs that assist parents in acquiring the knowledge, skill and direct help they need in child-rearing. Two types of community programs concern us in this discussion: (a) community service agencies that provide direct assistance and help: health, social and psychological services; (b) programs that provide specific information about child development and how parents directly can assist this development (i.e., parent education programs).

Community Service Agencies

Shipman (1977) followed a large group of mostly black Head Start children, from age 4 to 9. She found significant relationships between these children's cognitive and academic functioning and the family's connectedness to the community. Children who performed better on both types of measures at both ages 4 and 9 had mothers who used and were more knowledgeable about community resources, who designed a higher quality home learning environment, and who participated with the child in school-type activities at home. Likewise, mothers who were members of community groups (and who thus may have been more intricately linked to others in the community) had children who performed better academically. Shipman argued that:

> By providing differential opportunities for the parent's participation in society, there may be indirect effects upon the child via parental attitudes and childrearing behaviors acquired through such experiences (p. 17).

An additional study of Head Start provides further corroboration of the importance parents' community involvement may have for children's development (MIDCO, 1973). Parents who were highly involved in Head Start programs generally had children who made somewhat larger gains. These highly involved parents tended to be per-

sons who had been involved in community activities prior to their child's participation in Head Start.

Community institutions like churches and fraternal organizations provide services and support needed by many black families (Billingsley, 1968). Black parents who are able to link into the services provided by churches and organizations like the Elks, women's clubs, sororities and fraternities may secure scholarships for their children, food, clothing, jobs or legal advice—clearly a great variety of help for their children and family. Parents who identify those community agencies and programs which provide the type of sensitive assistance needed are likely to have children who prosper.

Parent Education Programs

Programs that have attempted to share with black parents relevant child development information and appropriate interaction strategies are *formal* family support systems, perhaps among our most effective ones to date. Those programs in which low-income black parents have been encouraged to use specific language, reinforcement and interaction patterns have made demonstrable changes in their young children's intellectual development and in parent behavior (Stevens, 1978). The most effective training programs for low-income black parents are those which (a) are prescriptive yet personalized; (b) continue for 18 to 24 months; (c) include systems of supervision and program monitoring; (d) are targeted squarely on both parent and child; and (e) allow the consultant to assume a secondary, supportive role.

REDESIGNING COMMUNITY PARENT SUPPORT SYSTEMS

Caution is in order. Frankly, we need substantially more research evidence that supports the hypothesis that parents' connectedness to friends, kin and institutions enables them to do a more skillful job of childrearing. The research reviewed here is largely suggestive of such a relationship, but it is indirect.

Nevertheless, the previous discussion has significant implications for how we conceptualize parent education programs. Black single families do not rear their children alone. Intact black families already draw upon friends, relatives and other sources for childrearing information. Parent educators will need to work with single parents and with intact families so that these linkages are enhanced rather than disrupted. Parent educators may need to involve significant members of a family network in the program, especially when the parent network is a tight, closely knit one. The parent educator or consultant may assist the parent in more skillfully identifying and using members of his or her family/friend network for information and help. Network members can be encouraged and assisted in providing help and assistance to the family. Programs planned in this "ecologically sensitive" manner may likely be more effective in the long term.

Greater diffusion of program benefits throughout the black community may be achieved by involving parents who are members of quite different networks. Some corroborative anecdotal data are available. Klaus and Gray (1968) observed that such diffusion of treatment effects did occur in the black community of a small southern town. There some black children were enrolled in a preschool program that also included a parent education component. They discovered that mothers whose children were not enrolled in the program but who were friends or relatives of target mothers began to learn and implement many of the techniques transmitted to the target mothers. These program mothers became consultants to others in their community; Klaus and Gray termed this "horizontal diffusion."

Certain types of education programs may enable parents to construct new social networks consisting of program participants. Programs that work with parents in groups rather than individually may well foster the development of new supplementary social networks. Observation of peer support groups like Alcoholics Anonymous and Weight Watchers corroborates their potency in sustaining changes in participant behavior. Programs that enable parents to construct such peer support or mutual help networks and use them in addition to the extended family may be more effective in the long run than programs that do not.

The extended family and circle of kin and friends are potent support systems for the black family. Societal support systems (parent education programs, health delivery systems, social and psychological service agencies) must be designed so that the "natural" support system used by black families is not disrupted. If these support systems can work in concert, child and parent development can only be enhanced.

References

Billingsley, A. *Black Families in White America.* Englewood Cliffs, NJ: Prentice-Hall, 1968.

Bronfenbrenner, U. *The Ecology of Human Development.* Cambridge, MA: Harvard University Press, 1979.

Furstenberg, F. *Unplanned Parenthood: Societal Consequences of Teenage Childbearing.* New York: Free Press, 1976.

Gutmann, H. *The Black Family in Slavery and Freedom, 1750-1925.* New York: Pantheon, 1976.

Hill, R. *Strengths of Black Families.* Washington, DC: National Urban League, 1972.

Johnson, A. S., and T. Ooms. "The Pressures of Government on Families." *Dimensions.* 9 (1980): 83-88.

Klaus, R. A., and S. W. Gray. "The Early Training Project for Disadvantaged Children: A Report After Five Years." *Monographs of the Society for Research in Child Development* 33 (1968). (Serial No. 120).

McAdoo, H.P. "Role of the Extended Family Support Network in the Maintenance of Stability and Mobility of Single and Married Black Mothers." Paper presented at conference, Support for Single-Parent Families Through Extended Family Networks, University of Notre Dame, South Bend, IN., May 1978.

MIDCO Educational Associates. "Investigation of the Effects of Parent Participation in Head Start." Final Technical Report. Denver, CO: MIDCO Educational Associates, 1973. (ERIC Document Id. No. ED 080 215)

Shipman, V.; J. D. McKee and B. Bridgeman. *Stability and Change in Family Status, Situation and Process Variables and Their Relationship to Children's Cognitive Performance.* Princeton, NJ: Educational Testing Service, 1977.

Sowell, T. *Essays and Data on American Ethnic Groups.* Washington, DC: The Urban Institute, 1978.

Stack, C. B. *All Our Kin.* New York: Harper, 1974.

Stevens, J.H., Jr. "Parent Education Programs: What Determines Effectiveness?" *Young Children* 33, 4 (May 1978): 59 -65.

———. "Teenage Mothers' Social Networks and Black Infant Development." Paper, Southeastern Conference on Human Development, Alexandria, VA, Apr. 1980.

Stressing the importance of teacher awareness in helping children cope with divorce, the authors suggest activities to develop positive self-images and better understanding of life in the "real world." Edie L. Whitfield is Assistant Professor and Kent Freeland, Associate Professor, School of Education, Morehead State University, Kentucky. Dr. Freeland is also Head of the Department of Curriculum and Instruction.

Divorce and Children
What Teachers Can Do

Edie L. Whitfield and Kent Freeland

MANY SOCIETAL PRESSURES are placed on children, but few have greater negative impact than the divorce of parents. Young children, innocent victims of divorce, learn to perceive themselves as abandoned misfits and residuals of a perfect lifestyle, the stereotyped "two-parent family." Teachers and other educators are unable to do anything directly about divorce rates, but they can and should do something to help children of divorced parents to make satisfactory adjustments. Aware teachers have many opportunities to dispel the social stigma, rejection and negative attitudes often associated with divorce and children from the so-called "broken home."

Taking an honest and realistic look at present-day society is perhaps a starting place for teachers. The age-old view of the "Norman Rockwell" household with a full-time working father, a stay-at-home mother and one or more school-age children reflects a mode of thinking that is passé in modern society. Like it or not, the divorce rate is on the rise with the prediction that some 50 percent of all children born in 1978 will live a portion of their lives in single-parent homes.* Divorce is a fact of life; it must be accepted and dealt with as a phenomenon of our modern age. As teachers become aware and seek to accept reality, they can assist children in many ways—both through an attitude approach to teaching and through planned activities within the curriculum to develop positive self-images and better understandings of life in the "real world." Some suggestions for teachers follow.

Attitude Approach to Teaching

☐ When family units are studied, as part of social studies or other disciplines, acknowledge the fact that there are many kinds of families: some with many children, others with only a few, still others with no children; some with grandparents; some with two parents and others with one.

☐ When bulletin boards and other exhibits or displays are planned depicting some phase of lifestyles (such as family breadwinners, careers, sports, etc.), include pictures showing female as well as male participants.

☐ Select children's literature to include broad ranges of settings from various lifestyles. Avoid an overabundance of "Norman Rockwell" households.

☐ Accept different lifestyles and customs children represent, and remember that children seldom control or choose their home lives.

☐ Focus projects and activities on the family, rather than on the mother or the father. When, for example, Mother's Day or Father's Day gifts are to be constructed as a class project, suggest that children select a female or a male in their family for whom they will design a gift. With such a flexible format, children are free to identify with their own particular lifestyle, and will not feel left out or different when others are making parental gifts.

---

* Janice J. Hammond, "Children, Divorce and You," *Learning* 9 (Feb. 1981): 83-89.

☐ Instead of "Parent Visitation Day," plan a "Visitors' Day." Children of working parents who cannot visit school during the day are then able to invite a neighbor or other family member to be their visitor. This avoids that left-out feeling when their parent or parents are unable to attend.

Planned Activities
Within the Curriculum

☐ Provide role-model activities that enable children to identify personally with various lifestyles and situations. While these activities can be planned as a part of many subjects, they are especially effective when utilized in social studies units.

☐ Plan reading and research projects that will serve two ends—development of reading and research skills and knowledge gained about the field being read or researched. Arrange research learning centers in the class-room. They will provide opportunities for children to make many interesting discoveries about the world in which they live.

☐ Assign as homework the viewing of care-fully selected television programs that provide opportunities for children to observe and iden-tify with various lifestyles and customs.

☐ Provide creative writing experiences to encourage children to replace old stereotyped story situations with some real-life patterns. *The Three Bears* could be rewritten to be a mother bear and two school-aged bear cubs. *Cinderella* could be depicted as having a happy life with her stepmother and stepsisters.

☐ When children are studying some period in history, suggest that they compare current statistics on divorce and working mothers with those of the era. In the process of comparing yesterday's and today's families, children not only learn many interesting facts but develop greater awareness of present-day lifestyles and societal change.

The Larger Question
Bilingual Education, Family and Society

Ida Santos Stewart

THE PURPOSE of bilingual education is currently the subject of great debate in the United States. A host of questions have been raised about bilingual education, its responsibility to families and its place in society. No one questions the fact that different families need different kinds of education—and for varied reasons. But what happens if families, bilingual education professionals and society differ in their perception of the goals of bilingual programs? How can this issue be resolved?

Bilingual education is, above all, a product of the two most important social structures of present-day society: the family and the school. To recognize the importance of bilingual education, it is necessary to understand the complex interaction of the family and the school within the larger society. This way of looking at bilingual education is useful in stimulating discussion that will, it is hoped, lead to clarification of some of the intricate issues surrounding bilingual education.

A Point of View

The enactment of the Bilingual Education Act of 1968, commonly known as Title VII of the Elementary and Secondary Education Act, recognized the need for bilingual-bicultural education. In response to this mandate and subsequent directives, bilingual programs were implemented essentially to provide educational programs that would raise the achievement level of students. Thirteen years later, innovative and effective bilingual programs continue to be difficult to initiate and nearly impossible to maintain.

One possible explanation is the lack of agreement on the purpose of bilingual education among bilingual educators, the family and the society. This view is based on three assumptions about bilingual education.

☐ First, it is assumed that solutions must and can be found for the educational deficiencies of bilingual students. The National Assessment of Educational Progress (1977) reported that Hispanic children tested consistently below the national average in reading, science, mathematics and social studies and repeated more grades than other children. In fact, for those Hispanic children with academic deficiencies, provision in kindergarten and 1st grade of bilingual education in their native language will not do. In a system that does not yet understand the needs of bilingual children, their educational problems are too complex to be solved with such a simplistic thrust.

It is, nevertheless, inconceivable that American society will continue to accept the failure of its schools to educate adequately such a large segment of its children. The United States has always been able to solve those problems it wants to solve; no time was wasted in the '60s in developing a successful space program. When the United States decides it wants equal educational opportunities for all of its children, it will provide the moral, educational and fiscal support. It can be done, but will it be done?

☐ The second assumption is that bilingual education to be effective must be re-

In clarifying some of the intricate issues surrounding bilingual education, Ida Santos Stewart takes the position that, to be effective, bilingual education programs must be responsive to family and society. The author is Associate Professor and Chairperson, Early Childhood Education Program, University of Houston, Texas.

sponsive to the family and the society. Believed to be the most powerful socializing influence, the family with its concern for the development of its children can, if it chooses, give direction and support to the school. Bilingual education must insist that the Hispanic family take its rightful place in the education of its children. With the information and support the family provides, the school can do a more effective job of preparing a positive learning environment in which bilingual children can realize their potential. The net effect of including parental values in the educational program is greater success in teaching Hispanic children. Both children and parents receive benefits only the school can provide.

But bilingual education must also respond to the larger society. The uncertainties generated by the debate between minority assimilation and minority assertion continue to multiply. Neither the larger society nor the bilinguals have resolved the question of assimilation. In the case of the Hispanic population, Spanish-speakers have been more resistant to assimilation than other ethnic enclaves in terms of retaining their language. Nevertheless, despite numerous obstacles, Hispanics are entering the larger society in significant numbers. As they do so, they are insisting on support measures to overcome society-imposed disadvantages. Bilingual education is one response of the society to provide equal educational opportunities while meeting the demands for ethnic integrity.

☐ The third assumption is that there is a range of possible solutions. Some programs stress the teaching of English. Unfortunately, this singular approach, often in the form of patterned drills of teaching English as a second language, ignores what the research literature tells us about how young children learn. Other approaches focus on understanding the children's culture to the exclusion of the requirement of effective teaching skills. And then there are those psychologically oriented approaches which are primarily concerned with personality development. This orientation ignores the fact that, to feel good about themselves in a school setting, children must be able to succeed academically. The bottom line is that the linkage among bilingual education, family and society is a social reality so encompassing that no single approach has the complete solution but all have a contribution to make. Those who attempt to address this relationship cannot do so without referring to constructs whose roots lie in such diverse fields as anthropology, linguistics and education.

Bilingual Education: A New Educational Perspective

In any attempt to understand the ties that bind the school to family and society, a few facts must be acknowledged. Over 400 million Americans, or about 16 percent of the people, speak a language other than English as a first language. Of these, over 12.1 million persons are of Spanish origin or descent (U.S. Bureau of the Census,

1980). Although precise data are not available, it is estimated that about 7 million children need special language programs. The need to respond to the educational needs of non-English speakers is great; yet, it is alarming to note, the schools are failing to educate bilingual children.

Although school failure has been acknowledged for many years, a decade of research on equal educational opportunities has shown that equal educational opportunities do not as yet exist for bilingual children. Jackson and Cosca (1974) identified a number of statistically significant pedagogical disparities in teacher behaviors directed toward Anglo and Chicano students. Such educational practices undoubtedly contribute to unequal educational opportunities which, in turn, are influencing factors in the low school attainment of bilingual students.

The needs of bilingual children differ from those of children from the larger society in important ways. Some Hispanic children arrive in school monolingual, speaking only Spanish; a number arrive bilingual, with Spanish dominant; others arrive bilingual, with English dominant. It is no accident that, regardless of their linguistic preferences, all these children are culturally bound to their rich Hispanic heritage by customs such as language, familial values, dress, diet and behavioral patterns. Gezi (1974) in his review of bilingual crosscultural research found that, all things being equal, bilingual children are comparable to Anglo monolingual children in their range of IQs and that school achievement tends to increase when the children's first language and cultural heritage are used in the instruction.

Educational programs must be designed to combat those aspects of schooling and society that prevent the biculturalism of children to be expressed. Such programs can assure that bilingual children will not join the larger society from a stance of hopelessness and powerlessness. Awareness of the bilingual, social and economic needs of children calls for new educational perspectives; it also calls for a new alliance of bilingual education, family and society.

What the Family Brings to Bilingual Education

The family can support the goals of the school by encouraging children to cooperate and to strive for achievement; it can, if it chooses to do so, conversely negate or neutralize the school's influence by belittling its efforts. Since the family is the children's first teacher and continues in this influential role for many years, bilingual education is more likely to be successful when the school and the family agree on the goals of schooling and the means whereby the goals will be achieved. But what if the family's perceptions of what bilingual education ought to be are not those of the bilingual program? One way to avoid this dilemma is to develop bilingual programs based upon the goals of parents for their children in conjunction with the knowledge and experience of bilingual educators.

Hispanic Family Profile Collaboration between family and school can begin with an understanding of the dimensions of the Hispanic family and its relationship to the children's schooling. The bilingual family has often been cited as the primary cause of its children's low school achievement. Along with the centrality of the family unit and the assumed resultant lack of individual initiative, the bilingual family is faulted with a resistance to change. However, a comprehensive review of census data produced a demographic profile of the Hispanic family which documents both persistence and change in family life patterns (U.S. Bureau of the Census, 1980).

Evidence on Hispanic families suggests that extended family households in the traditional mode are increasingly rare, that the supportive mutual obligations of the extended family have diminished, and that a high rate of divorce and separation is changing the traditional family structure. The Hispanic family has lost some of its family solidarity and re-defined its ties to the surrounding community. Nevertheless, unlike the Anglo family, it has not entirely cast off its extended family norms. An extensive network of mutual aid among relatives continues to be a strong family feature, and fulfillment of family obligations remains an influencing factor.

Hispanic Maternal Teaching Style In the Hispanic family, mothers are usually responsible for care of the children. Steward and Steward (1973) studied how Anglo, Chicano and Chinese American mothers taught a sorting and motor-skills game to their preschool sons. As expected, the single best predictor of maternal teaching style and child response was ethnicity. As teachers, Chicano mothers made greater use of nonverbal instructions and included a higher percentage of original adult wording than Anglo or Chinese mothers.

Interestingly, in the teaching episodes, the Chicano mother continued to see her role as that of mother rather than teacher. For example, one mother in explaining her teaching style stated, "The schools do that." Kindergarten teachers also reported differential maternal school expectations. In leaving her child at school, the Chinese mother is inclined to say, "If my son doesn't learn what he should, let me know"; the Chicano mother wants to be called if her son misbehaves.

Hispanic Familial Education Norms Contrary to expectations, Hispanic students have been found to come from families where education is stressed. Children are encouraged to do well in school. On the whole, bilingual parents readily acknowledge the fact that they are dependent on the school to teach their children specific academic skills which are essential for success in adulthood. Considering the parents' limited access to school, it is significant that school activities are topics of family discussions. Of particular interest is the fact that, more often than not, parents speak of the benefits their children will accrue as the result of schooling rather than the inadequacies of their children's education.

School and Family Cooperation

Despite professions of good will, most bilingual programs have not sufficiently incorporated parent expectations for their children's schooling. Certainly, one characteristic of an effective bilingual program is the level of cooperation and communication between school and family. Unquestionably, open communication between teachers and parents can go a long way in clarifying misconceptions and generating support for the program.

To develop a close collaboration, nothing is so successful as personal communication between school personnel and the family. Most often the contact person is the teacher. During the first parent-teacher conference, held either in the home or at the school, teachers play a dual role: as learners they have the opportunity to become attuned to the life of the family; as professionals they begin to build a relationship based on accessibility and trust. This is the time for parents and teachers to discuss their expectations, for the teachers to share their plans for the year and for the parents to verbalize their expectations for their children's schooling. There is no substitute for first-hand knowledge of the family in understanding the parameters within which a bilingual program must operate.

Once the channels of communication are established, the school needs to continue to support parent and family participation. Family members may have special talents that can be used to advantage with children in school. Older members may be the source of the history or traditions of the family and community. Building on the strong helping relationships within the bilingual family, cross-age tutoring can be initiated. Bilingual education thus becomes a mutual undertaking.

Regular room meetings, as well as school-wide meetings, can be held to report progress, concerns and needs. Information can also be disseminated through letters written in English or Spanish, as needed, or telephone calls which are both more personal and direct. Yet another means of communication would be to have family members participate in classroom activities with the children. The purpose of these collaborations would be to keep families apprised of the current status of their children and the school's efforts to provide quality education.

Perhaps no aspect of parent involvement has received as much attention and thought as parent advisory councils. While everyone agrees that parent involvement is needed, seldom have parent councils been successful. Parent councils have failed for these reasons: (1) advisory councils are often bereft of power, so that parents learn not to waste their time and efforts on meaningless participation; (2) school personnel tend to consider themselves "the experts," thus placing parents in the dependent role of deferring to them for solutions to schooling problems. When the parents are from a minority group, the problems are compounded even further.

Without a doubt, the most important problems affecting the schooling of bilingual children are those associated with the variance between the value systems of the school and the family. On the one hand, parents want their children to have the education they lack; on the other hand, they know that if schooling is successful it will initiate irreversible changes in their children. Inevitably, familial values will be in conflict with newly acquired school values. Bilingual education can be there to help both the children and their parents resolve this conflict so that family and societal needs can be met.

The Momentum of Society

For the bilingual population, the overriding problem has been to keep their culture intact and meaningful in the face of their desire for participation in the larger society. This desire has been tempered by their inability to achieve equality in the economic world and society's resistance to accepting them socially and politically.

In regard to ethnic plurality in education, Americans took a moral stand in 1968 when they enacted the Bilingual Education Act which recognized the need of special assistance for those children whose dominant language was not English. Perhaps even more important was the Supreme Court *Lau vs. Nichols* decision of 1974 which held that schools receiving federal funds could not discriminate against children of limited or non-English speaking ability by denying them language training.

Although the status of English as the official language of the U.S. has never been in question, bilingualism in education can no longer be ignored. The collective conscience of the people has recognized contrasting styles of living within the society as well as beyond it.

Preparing for the '80s

The foregoing review of the relationship among bilingual education, the family and the larger society has provided **few unequiv-**

ocal answers. Not only is there uncertainty about the data, but many critical issues remain untouched. Nevertheless, these analyses may serve to highlight a few developments that have implications for the future.

In the matrix of bilingual education, family and society, each has a unique function and each is influenced by the other. Of course, conflicts of purpose and function arise as each asserts its identity and views bilingual education in terms of its own perceived needs. Nevertheless, in spite of underlying conceptual differences, all three have made a commitment to the education of bilingual children. Out of this commitment one of the most notable educational and moral achievements of the '80s can emerge.

The decade of the '70s was a painful period of beginning educational opportunities for non-English speaking children; the '80s will be the decade when Spanish speakers no longer will be disproportionately represented among the poorly educated. The Hispanics are ready to enjoy the privileges and assume the responsibilities of American citizenship.

References

Gezi, K. "Bilingual-Bicultural Education: A Review of Relevant Research." *California Journal of Educational Research* 25, 5 (Nov. 1974): 233-29.

Jackson, G., and C. Cosca. "The Inequality of Educational Opportunity in the Southwest: An Observational Study of Ethnically Mixed Classrooms." *American Educational Research Journal* 11, 3 (Summer 1974): 219-29.

National Assessment of Educational Progress. National Center of Education Statistics, May 20, 1977, ERIC Index.

Steward, M., and D. Steward. "The Observation of Anglo-Mexican and Diverse-American Mothers Teaching Their Young Sons." *Child Development* 44 (1973): 329-37.

U.S. Bureau of the Census. *Current Population Reports, Population Characteristics, Population Profile of the United States,* 1979. Washington, DC: Government Printing Office, May 1980.

Jerome Leavitt pleads with teachers to accept responsibility for helping to eradicate a social cancer. He provides much-needed information for teachers and others who work with children. The author has conducted almost 100 workshops and classes on the subject of child abuse and neglect. He is Professor of Education and Child Abuse at California State University, Fresno.

Helping Abused and Neglected Children

Jerome E. Leavitt

CHILDREN IN THE UNITED STATES don't "have it as good" as most people think. Approximately 2 million children are abused and neglected in the United States each year and more than 2,000 of them end up dying. It is estimated that one out of every 10 children is physically abused, physically neglected, sexually abused or psychologically abused/neglected. The amount of abuse and neglect in each state is probably proportionate: a teacher may have two or more such children in his/her classroom this year. Indeed, the problem of child abuse and neglect cuts across all economic, ethnic, religious, vocational and social lines.

Child abuse and neglect are on the increase, even taking into account the fact that better detection and reporting on the part of teachers produces larger figures. To do their part, teachers need to know their state laws and how to recognize and report abuse and neglect. They also need to know how they can work with children and parents who have this problem. In the case of abuse and neglect, we are talking about what happens to children as a result of the act of parents or guardians.

THE LAW AND REPORTING

Although every state has a law requiring the reporting of child abuse and neglect, the laws vary enough so that we cannot give them here. Teachers should contact their school principal or superintendent for a copy of the state laws as they relate to teachers and for information on the reporting procedure for their school district. If the school does not have the information, it may be secured directly from the office of the state district attorney. In practically every state, teachers can be held legally responsible for any damage to a child caused by their failure to report suspected abuse and neglect. And, of course, they are protected against being sued for reporting.

Many states require that teachers report orally and in writing all cases of suspected child abuse and neglect within a specific length of time to their local law enforcement agency and/or children's protective services. It is generally considered that teachers can, within a reasonable degree, distinguish between children's accidents and abuse and neglect.

IDENTIFYING SUSPECTED ABUSE AND NEGLECT

Teachers are responsible for reporting when, in their judgment, a child is likely to have been abused or neglected; they don't have to prove it. Those in the legal, social work and/or medical professions will take it from there.

Physical Abuse
Many children are physically abused in the guise of discipline: they are bruised,

27

wounded, fractured, cut or brain damaged in an ill-attempted effort to make them "shape up"; that is, obey the parent or caretaker. Others are burned with a hot liquid by immersion or placed on a heater in an attempt to force toilet-training.

Physical abuse may be suspected when the child has:

☐ bruises that could not possibly happen during play
☐ bruises that are found on more than one side of the body
☐ bruises that show patterns from a belt buckle or coat hanger
☐ bruises of different coloration that occurred at different times
☐ bruises that are clustered
☐ bruises on the back of the body where a child does not fall
☐ or bruises that are inconsistent with the age of the child.

Burns are somewhat more difficult to evaluate. They show up as abuse if they are caused by cigarettes, rope or immersion. Dry burns may signal that a child has been forced to sit or place his/her hands on a flame or heater.

Physical Neglect

Some abuse is passive, such as neglect when children:

☐ are abandoned
☐ lack supervision
☐ are not fed properly
☐ need medical or dental care
☐ are frequently late for school or absent
☐ do not have appropriate or sufficient clothing
☐ have bodies that are unclean
☐ or live in unsafe or filthy homes.

These children need as much help as their counterparts who are physically abused.

Sexual Misuse

Educators are only now becoming aware of the sexual misuse of both younger and older children. This is much harder to detect than physical abuse or neglect because there are no outward signs. Children are subjected to every known sexual act from fondling to intercourse even before they are old enough to go to school—sometimes continually until they become adults. In some cases they are sold or rented as prostitutes and used to make kiddy porno films. However, with both very young and older children there are behavioral indicators that give us clues in identification.

At this point we need to mention that both boys and girls are subjected to sexual abuse and need to be considered equally vulnerable. Sexual misuse may be suspected when very young children:

☐ cannot sit on play equipment
☐ squirm in their chairs
☐ straddle-walk as if their pants are wet
☐ or touch or manipulate their clothes around the genital areas.

However, a large portion of these children will have other conditions that cause these actions such as boils, rashes or tight clothes. In any event, such children need help; the school nurse should be contacted for a follow-up.

With older children, the clues will be verbal. The child may confide in the teacher with statements to the effect: "I am afraid to go home." "Can I come and live with you?" Or, "How can I become adopted?" The teacher should probe to see what the child really has in mind. Chances are the child will confide in the teacher, regardless of the latter's sex. In fact, children sometimes feel freer to confide in a teacher of the opposite sex.

Psychological Abuse/Neglect

The most harmful, and probably the most prevalent, abuse of children today is in the psychological area. The effects of this type of abuse on a child often carry over into adulthood. Psychological abuse takes the form of either doing something harmful to the child or withholding something desirable from the child.

Children are hurt directly when parents:
- [ ] are inconsistent in talk, rules or actions
- [ ] impose unreasonable scholastic standards on them
- [ ] use them in marital battles
- [ ] engage in belittling and blaming them
- [ ] or regularly use sarcasm.

Indirectly, children can be hurt when parents:
- [ ] do not show physical affection for them
- [ ] do not take an interest in any of their activities
- [ ] converse with them in a "cold" manner
- [ ] emotionally starve them
- [ ] or withhold praise of any kind.

While psychological abuse is difficult to trace, its effects are all too evident in the classroom.

WHO ARE THE ABUSERS?

The discussion so far has focused on the types of child abuse and neglect and on identification. Now a few words about the people who do these things to children. Contrary to popular belief, people from low-income families are not the major abusers. Abuse and neglect occur in all economic, cultural, racial and social groups and to about the same degree. The number of child abusers who are psychotic or psychopathic is small, between 10 and 20 percent. The rest are as rational as you or I, except for this one point—they are child abusers. Frequently abusing parents experienced deficient childhoods; probably about 80 percent of the people who abuse children were abused themselves as children, in the same form.

The persons who are abusers tend not only to come from abusive and neglectful families but to experience many problems themselves: poor self-image, lack of self-confidence, immaturity, incompetence, depression, hostility, alcoholism and drug addiction. A high percentage never learned how to be adequate parents and how to discipline properly.

HELPING CHILD AND PARENTS

In severe cases of suspected child abuse and neglect, the teacher has the legal and moral obligation to report the situation to the appropriate authorities. In cases where children are having problems that are minor in nature, teachers can help directly or through the assistance of the school principal, nurse and/or social worker. When sexual misuse is suspected, reporting is the only legal or ethical procedure. In cases involving overly severe discipline but not physical abuse, the teacher can work with both the child and the parent to help develop a better relationship between the two and offer alternative ways of discipline to the parent. Invite such parents to the classroom to see how you handle discipline problems.

In non-major cases of neglect, especially in the areas of body cleanliness, clothing and eating, older children can be taught how to care for themselves. Here, again, under certain conditions teachers can help parents to be better at parenting through group discussions and individual counseling.

Psychological abuse is the one area in which very little is known or done to help the child. Agencies in general stay clear of this area unless it is combined with one of the other three. This is probably the area in which teachers and other school professionals can make the greatest contribution in a direct manner. As in the area of discipline, teachers and others can help parents to improve their parenting skills by helping them understand the necessity to be consistent, fair and concerned. Parents can be helped to understand that each child in the family needs quality time with the parents each day. As for the children, it is vital that the teacher help them to develop a good self-image and to "fit" into the classroom and be part of the group. With a strong self-image, a child is in a good position to combat many adverse situations.

CONCLUSIONS

In the push to concentrate on the "basics," we need to re-think our priorities: we cannot teach a dead or physically or psychologically abused child. Teachers must accept responsibility for helping to eliminate and prevent child abuse and neglect. Education is the first step. The bibliography and reference sources that follow will be helpful in this regard. Some of these materials are also appropriate for parents. Teachers are urged to request that both their town and school libraries purchase them.

Abuse can be eliminated in part by reporting suspected cases, as indicated. Abuse can be prevented in part by breaking the cycle through education of the present generation of parents and the children who will be the parents of tomorrow.

Sources of Information

Anne Cohn, Executive Director, National Committee for Prevention of Child Abuse, 111 E. Wacker Dr., Suite 510, Chicago, IL 60601.

Wayne Holder, Associate Director, Child Protection, The American Humane Association, 5351 S. Roselyn St., Denver, CO 80110.

C. D. Jones, Associate Director, Child Abuse Project, Education Commission of the States, Suite 300, 1860 Lincoln St., Denver, CO 80295.

Leonard Lieber, National Administrator, Parents Anonymous, 22330 Hawthorne Blvd., Suite 208, Torrance, CA 95050.

Joan Solheim, Education Director, National Center for the Prevention and Treatment of Child Abuse and Neglect, 4200 E. 9th Ave., Denver, CO 80262.

Bibliography

Association for Childhood Education International. "Protecting Children: Freeing Them from Mental and Physical Abuse."*Childhood Education* 52, 2 (Nov./Dec. 1975).

Fontana, Vincent J. *Somewhere a Child Is Crying.* New York: Macmillan, 1973.

Gil, David G. *Violence Against Children.* Cambridge, MA: Harvard University Press, 1970.

Giovannoni, Jeanne M., and Rosina M. Becerra. *Defining Child Abuse.* New York: Free Press, 1979.

Halperin, Michael. *Helping Maltreated Children.* St. Louis: C. V. Mosby, 1979.

Helfer, Ray E., and Henry C. Kempe. *The Battered Child.* Chicago: University of Chicago Press, 1974.

———. *Child Abuse and Neglect: The Family and Community.* Cambridge, MA: Ballinger, 1976.

Leavitt, Jerome E. *The Battered Child: Selected Readings.* New York: General Learning Press, 1974.

Martin, Harold P. *The Abused Child.* Cambridge, MA: Ballinger, 1976.

O'Brien, Shirley. *Child Abuse: A Crying Shame.* Provo, UT: Brigham Young University Press, 1980.

Polansky, Norman A., et al. *Roots of Futility.* San Francisco, CA: Jossey-Bass, 1972.

Straus, Murray A., et al. *Behind Closed Doors.* Garden City, NY: Anchor Press, 1980.

Wooden, Kenneth. *Weeping in the Playtime of Others.* New York: McGraw-Hill, 1976.

Editor's note: The author has offered to put you in touch with additional resource material, specialists in your area who can help you with your problems, or training courses that deal with the tragedy of the battered and neglected child. Write to Dr. Jerome E. Leavitt, 39736 Pineridge Way, Oakhurst, CA 93644.

Libby Vernon puts parenting in perspective as she reviews the history of child-rearing. She then offers some guidelines for effective parenting. The author is Principal of Jess Harben Elementary School, Richardson Independent School District, Texas.

Putting Parenting in Perspective

Libby Vernon

IN CENTURIES PAST, parenting was a spontaneous response to the biological phenomenon of birth and received little conscious thought or planning. It served an economic purpose as well as an emotional one. Financially secure families of all nations had fixed customs of inheritance; therefore, much of child-rearing centered on preparing offspring to assume the responsibility appropriate to their position within the family's economic framework. While the wealthy nobility used parenting as an opportunity to maintain wealth and social status, the less fortunate and less affluent families used it as a means of augmenting or achieving economic stability. In a primarily agrarian society, more children meant more hands to aid in the tasks of production.

As the world became more technologically oriented, children were expected to contribute financially to the family. Consequently, some became victims of the horrors of child labor in factories and mines. Parents' emotional relationship with their children, moreover, was intimately tied to their need for someone to care for them as they became too old and weak to care for themselves. Thus, the golden era of the extended family evolved not only because of strong affection and a loving desire for many offspring but also because of the absence of alternatives.

The baby boom following World War II reflected a dramatic societal change—an effort to right a world gone awry. Parenting provided an opportunity to re-enter a period of normalcy, a period of creating and nurturing

This is an adaptation of Dr. Vernon's address at the 1981 ACEI Study Conference in Little Rock, Arkansas.

life rather than destroying it. The affluence of society, coupled with tremendous strides in technology, produced the first generation of children who were chosen and cherished simply for "being." As this generation matured, an entirely new philosophy of parenting emerged. For the first time, child-care specialists devoted more space to the affective area of parent-child relationships than to the nutritional and custodial aspects.

Parents eagerly followed the guidance of experts. Consequently, assuming the role of disciplinarian threatened many parents who feared that the effects of harsh, corporal punishment in childhood would psychologically cripple their children in adulthood. Women's magazines, in turn, carried myriad articles instructing mothers how to devote themselves totally to their children.

Children who had been traditionally involved in the tasks of maintaining a home and producing a living were now replaced by machines. Mothers no longer taught daughters the best way to make soap or preserve foods, and fathers now worked in environments that excluded children. Child-rearing became almost an exclusively female ritual. Conversely, fathers of the era were exhorted to become buddies with their sons: to spend time with them playing baseball or fishing. Getting socially acquainted with children became a major paternal role, and all too often mothers became social "servants." They organized car pools and became cub scout leaders, PTA activists and child study club members. For the first time in history, the opportunities for parenting became an entire lifestyle.

31

The 1970s revealed a time of re-examination of this unprecedented parental role. Women's magazines included articles encouraging parents to develop communication with their children and to exercise caution in becoming too involved in out-of-home activities. Some pointed out that other youngsters, rather than fathers, fulfill the role of buddies and that fathers should now take the responsibility of modeling acceptable adult behavior for both their sons and daughters. The '70s saw child-rearing and children acknowledged.

As we enter the '80s, we find many changes in society—and none more challenging than parenting. The increasing number of mothers who work outside the home poses perhaps the most dramatic change in the family pattern. Inflation, increased education of women and institutionalized day care have all contributed to this change. Better career opportunities for women, together with the expectation of many husbands that wives will contribute both intellectually and financially to the family, have also greatly affected family lifestyles.

Families that include a homebound mother and a father who works from 8:00 to 5:00 are now in the minority. For instance, many fathers' work requires that they travel frequently, and more than 50 percent of U.S. mothers work outside the home. Many two-parent families have modified the traditional pattern to meet their unique needs.

Perhaps the most significant factor affecting today's society is contraception, which can be practiced at reasonable cost with minimal health hazard. Children are more likely to be the product of parental choice, not chance. Consequently, parents are better able to prepare for the responsibilities of parenthood both emotionally and financially.

Another factor profoundly affecting the family is that of divorce. The dissipation of much of the social stigma associated with divorce and women's increased ability to provide financially for themselves and their children have contributed to the increased divorce rate. Single parenting has become an established role in society and, although a majority of single parents are mothers, it is no longer unusual to find fathers functioning in this role. Despite the rapid increase of single parents, the response of services and facilities to single-parent needs has been relatively sluggish. Complete acceptance of the single-parent home as a healthful nurturing environment for child-

rearing has yet to be realized. Nonetheless, the pervasive presence of the single-parent family dictates that schools, community service organizations and religious institutions alter attitudes to include this alternative.

Still another factor affecting family lifestyles is that of the blended family. The pattern itself is not new. In times past, the shorter life expectancy of women predisposed men to having more than one wife and family. What is new in today's blended family pattern is the factor of divorce. Often a divorced person remarries and chooses to have more children. This mix of children from more than one marriage challenges those organizations which serve children's needs and support parents' child-rearing efforts.

Today, more than ever before, we must try to glean the positive aspects of child-rearing practices throughout history. Necessity compels us to combine our feelings with our knowledge and experience as we assume the important responsibility of child-rearing. The guidelines that follow should prove useful:

☐ Discipline that teaches a child self-control and enhances the feeling of competency is indispensable and, when administered consistently and fairly, becomes a stabilizing force in the child's life.

☐ High expectations based upon a child's real talents and abilities open the way to self-fulfillment for the child. Consistent parental support and encouragement help a child realize his or her full potential.

☐ Mature, loving and consistent adult modeling behavior provides a mirror in which children see and measure themselves. Parents must willingly acknowledge to their children their shortcomings as well as their strengths, so that one day their children will be able to do likewise.

☐ When children view parents in roles outside the home, they gain a perspective of parents as productive individuals in the community rather than as extensions of themselves.

In rearing children, parents are shaping the society of the future. How appropriate, then, is Abraham Lincoln's advice:

There is someone who will one day fill your place in society. [That person] will manage your businesses, administer your governments, and determine the destiny of your world. The care which you give to them today will mold the destiny of your old age for they will give your care back to you. They are our children.

"As parents or parenting-people, we must be aware of what causes stress in a particular child and of the importance of offering relief or of eliminating the cause as much as possible."

Gladys Gardner Jenkins is Lecturer in Parent-Child-Teacher Relationships, University of Iowa, Iowa City.

For Parents Particularly

Gladys Gardner Jenkins

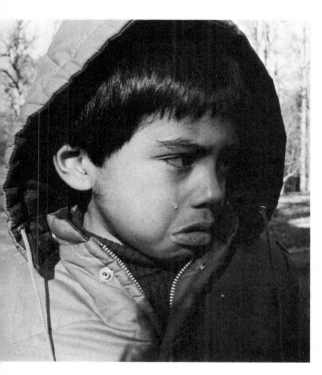

WE LIKE to think of the years of childhood as happy years. We do *not* like to think that children may be anxious, fearful or faced with circumstances that are filled with stress. Far too often we tend to push aside the feelings of children, failing to realize that some situations, which may not seem of great concern to us, may be of deep concern to them. How often we say, "He'll grow out of it," "She'll get over it," or "Run along now; that's nothing to be afraid of."

Parents have written to me from time to time about some of their concerns:

☐ "Beth can't stand competitive games. Her teacher tells me that even something like musical chairs worries the child dreadfully. She feels that at six Beth is old enough to learn how to accept competition, but both at home and at school she bursts into tears whenever she loses."

☐ "Jacob came home from school in tears today. All the first-grade children had been given a standardized test. He was sure he had failed because he could not answer all the questions. He sobbed, "I'm scared to go back to school—my teacher will be mad; she likes me to get things right.""

☐ "Our Pat is small for his age and does not have good coordination. He just isn't an athlete, but his father is determined that he be 'all man.' He is pushing him into Little League; he yells at him from the sidelines and keeps him working at ball and bat at home. Pat can't take the pressure; and when he bursts into tears, his father turns from him in anger."

☐ "Jon is seriously upset and having nightmares. He is becoming aggressive at home, hitting out and throwing things. We could not understand what had come over him until we just found out that a group of big boys have been threatening to hurt the smaller ones. One of their threats was, 'Don't dare tell anyone or we'll kill you!' We only found out because one of the small boys broke down and told his parents. One of the disturbing things to me about Jon's distress is that even now he honestly doesn't know what was real, dreams or fantasy about this. When he tries to talk about it, he ends up saying he doesn't know whether it really happened or not—and then he runs off. He won't play outdoors anymore."

☐ "Greta's grandmother just died. We did take her to the funeral. Her teacher is concerned because now Greta plays 'burying' at recess time, and all her pictures are of coffins and funerals."

☐ "I've just been divorced and I am disturbed because my ten-year-old son Paul barely speaks to me. The other day he shouted at me, 'I'm just angry, plain angry, with you and Dad!'"

Winners and Losers

Beth's teacher was right that Beth needed to learn how to meet competition, but she was obviously not able to do so. Her teacher recommended that the family increase the number of competitive games they played, so Beth could get used to both winning and losing. What seemed a good idea actually made the situation worse. Beth continued to burst into tears, throw down the cards, knock the pieces off the board, and run out of the room. She was already in too competitive a situation, for her two older brothers were always able to win. Already at six she was thinking of herself as a "loser." Losing had happened too often to her and had become too much to cope with. When a child is unable to cope, it is important to look backward and try to discover what experiences he or she has had that may be blocking forward growth.

Jacob came from a family with high standards for his performance. His parents were proud of his intelligence; and his teacher, recognizing his ability, expected him to do well in school. He had had little experience with what he felt was failure. When he met it, he did not know how to cope. He equated acceptance with success. Bright children can feel as anxious about failure as children of less ability, particularly if they are subjected to pressures to always succeed. Both Jacob's parents and teacher will need to lessen their pressures. Jacob will also need some healthy experiences with situations in which he does not always do well. Far too much pressure is probably exerted if a child feels that he must always succeed. Such a child will have difficulties learning to cope with reality.

Reality and Nightmare

Jon, who had been a healthy seven-year-old, had been faced with a seriously traumatic experience, so much so that reality and nightmare had become woven together. His behavior changed as he tried to fight off his fears. His fears increased so that whenever he saw big boys he, who had once played with children of many ages, began to run and hide and refuse to go out to play. Jon's parents realized that he could not handle this stressful experience alone. They also realized that he might need professional help to work it through. Changes in Jon's behavior—often the first indication that a child is under stress—alerted his parents to the fact that something serious had disturbed him.

Family Crises

Pat's mother had a difficult family situation to try to work out. Pat is under extreme and mounting pressure from his father who has only one goal in mind—to keep Pat from being a "sissy" and turn him into "all man." It is doubtful whether the father will easily change his position. If he does not do so, Pat is likely to crumple under the pressure. He will become increasingly fearful of his father and aliented from him. Such continuing stress is more than a child can meet. Since the mother is aware of the situation, she can try to build up Pat's confidence in other areas. His present picture of himself as a "no good" boy is indeed sad, for one of the qualities a child needs to develop if the stresses of life can be met is that of self-confidence.

When children are faced with a family crisis such as divorce, they may show their feelings by disturbed behavior, poor school work, withdrawal into themselves, or even anger (as Paul did). Yet so often the feelings of the children in such stressful times either go unrecognized or are pushed aside because the adults are emotionally involved in their own crises. The splitting apart of a family is a period of great stress for most children. Few children can cope with divorce without the help and understanding support of their parents or of other adults who have insight into the depth of feelings involved, as a child must try to cope with mixed loyalties and adjust to living in a one-parent home.

Similarly, if the family crisis is death, awareness is needed that the children in the family may be under as much stress as the adult members. Greta was acting out her anxieties about the death of her grandmother. These may have been concerned not only with missing a loved grandmother, but with all the feelings about death that may have surged up in the little girl. Death can be deeply perplexing and disturbing to a child. So much is not understood. Acting these feelings out as Greta sought to do, through painting and play, could be a healthy release helping her to come to terms with what had happened; but she would also need understanding grownups who would not criticize her or tell her not to "play that game." She would need help in thinking through the meaning of death and of a funeral, how it related to her and to the other grownups she loved. As a child is helped to talk about feelings that prompted the acting out, it is possible to begin to learn how to cope.

More Cues for Coping

Some children can cope better with stress than others. A child who is secure at both home and school has a base from which to face normal stresses. Such a child knows that if things are too hard to take, if the hurts go deep, the feelings, anxieties and concerns can be talked over and shared with parents and with teachers. But a child already insecure and anxious, or unsure about love and support at home, may not have developed the needed confidence and inner strength to be able to cope with any added stress. A child who is faced with the loss of a parent, or who is growing up in a home in which the emotional climate is unpredictable, may be faced with such continual stress and uncertainty that learning to cope is beyond his or her capacity.

How We Can Help

We can help our children to learn to cope with stress by showing our approval when they handle a situation that was difficult for them to meet, thus building their self-confidence. We can keep our expectations within reasonable limits so that our children can have opportunities to be successful problem-solvers. We can be good listeners so that our children can share with us those things that bother them.

We need to be aware, also, that the ways we handle our own feelings and actions in times of stress will indeed influence how our children learn to cope with stress. If we go to pieces when our child is faced with a difficult situation (such as both Jon and Pat experienced), if in times of death or divorce or family tragedy we let our own emotions spill over on to the children without the counter-force of talking with them and comforting them, our children will have real difficulty in facing strain.

As our children grow, it is essential that we help them to learn how to cope with stress, for some stress will be inevitable in their lives. At the same time we need to be observant of the behavior signals they send to us when stressful experiences are *beyond* their ability to cope. As parents or parenting people, we must be aware of what causes stress in a particular child and of the importance of offering relief or of eliminating the cause as much as possible. Too much continuing stress is defeating to any child. If relief is not possible—as it might not be in the case of a severe handicap, a family tragedy or a serious family crisis—we must help the child to live with stress through our continued strengthening support and encouragement.

Whatever Happened to Home Sweet Home?

Shirley O'Brien

ON THE LEFT you see George, father and provider for this lovely family. The woman next to him is his wife, Marie, mother and co-provider. Next to her is 13-year-old Debbie, a dyed-in-the-wool Kiss fan; to her left is Cheryl, almost 12 and crazy about the Rolling Stones and Chicago. Ten-year-old Ken is hooked on television.

Let's take a closer look at this family. Why does father George have high blood pressure? Why is mother Marie getting gray? Why do daughters Debbie and Cheryl always play their rock music so much? So loud? Why is son Ken always glued to the TV set?

Why? Because this family is changing! Debbie, Cheryl and Ken are caught up in the change process called adolescence. But Mom and Dad are changing too. In fact, as their firstborn reaches adolescence, George and Marie may be making more changes than Debbie, Cheryl and Ken put together. These changes mean storm and stress . . . crisis. Why?

Some of the answers can be found in the very word *adolescence*. In the original Latin it means "becoming." Adolescence is the process of "becoming" an adult. Anyone who spends time around teens participates in the crises of becoming.

CRISIS AREAS FOR ADOLESCENTS

What are major crisis areas for teens?

(1) The *media* represent one force that produces crisis in George and Marie's family. Since the media come from the outside, they can be controlled and tamed with proper action. For example, George and Marie can help their children realize the effects of TV, rock music and movies on communication and activities. But what about the inner forces that produce crisis? What are they? How can they be controlled and tamed?

(2) The most obvious internal crisis for the adolescent is *body change*. Spending hours in front of the mirror, teens try to read their bodies. They ask such questions as: "Am I too fat?" "Too thin?" "Are my breasts big enough?" "Is my penis the right size?" "Do I have the right amount of hair in the right places?" "Are my freckles too small?" "My pimples too large?" "My voice too low . . . too high?" "Do I match up with my friends?" In the shower after gym class, comparisons take place in the form of secretive, sidelong glances. The size, shape and function of the adolescents' bodies are changing; and for most of them, time moves so slowly.

Shirley O'Brien explains that adolescence is the process of "becoming" an adult. She contends that "Anyone who spends time around teens participates in the crises of 'becoming'." The author is Human Development Specialist at the Cooperative Extension Service, University of Arizona, Tucson.

EVERYONE
is in a period
of change

they go or what they do, they believe people are watching them. Even when alone, they tend to perform for this imaginary audience.

The egocentric half of them says: "You are special, you are different, you are unique. Things that happen to others will never happen to you because you are so wonderfully unusual. Everyone is concerned with the way you walk, what you wear, how you behave. You are performing on the stage of life!"

The other half of their self says: "You don't even know who you are or what you can do! You may not succeed or be liked; you may not have any friends."

Cheryl's self-doubt side sounds like this: "Oh, Mother, I'm so worried about the dance Saturday night! What if no one dances with me? What if I'm wearing the wrong thing? What if I don't know anyone? What if I don't know how to act?" Mom lovingly says: "Cheryl, whatever you do, act *natural.* You're a nice girl; you'll do just fine. Just act yourself!" And Cheryl says: "Oh, Moth—er! You always say that. How can I act myself when I don't even know who I am? Don't you think I would act like myself if I knew how *myself* would act?" And so it goes. The self-doubts are constantly telling Cheryl she may not succeed; yet, on the other hand, Cheryl feels quite special and different from everyone else.

To complicate the crises, every teen develops at a different rate. Even when teens are exactly the same age, there can be great differences in body size and development.

Another complication: girls mature more quickly than boys and, even though they may be the same age and grade in school, their interests can be as different as night and day.

(3) Another internal crisis is *self-discovery.* Teens ask these questions: "Who am I?" "What can I do?" "Whom do I need?" "Who needs me?" "Who should my friends be?" In this process of becoming, they are constantly trying to balance their feelings of self-doubt and their feelings of egocentricity—preoccupation with themselves.

Often teens imagine that others are as concerned with them as they are with themselves. They construct what might be called an *imaginary audience.* No matter where

Unfortunately, egocentric feelings enter when teens take chances with their lives. For example, when the boy who plays "chicken" on his motorbike hits a tree, he finds it hard to believe it really happened to him. The girl who gets pregnant says: "I didn't think it could ever happen to me! I'm the only *good* girl this has ever happened to!" Egocentric feelings and self-doubts confuse and bewilder teens.

(4) A fourth internal crisis is caused by the *need for independence*, the urge to break away—to become an adult. Parents have to "play it by ear." They find themselves dealing with an immature child one minute and a responsible adult the next. One of parents' most difficult tasks is adjusting to this unpredictability.

Parents are not the only ones having a difficult time adjusting to independence. A 16-year-old boy summed it up this way:

"I'm caged, locked up! I sit in school all day and study subjects that bore me. I'd like to work with my hands but I'm told I have to 'get ahead,' be somebody important. My parents are always worrying about whom I'm going out with—is she a good girl, and will we be good, or will there be trouble. They say they know I'm grown up, but they don't really believe it. They tell me it's because they love me that they worry; but they worry most, I've noticed, when I'm off doing something on my own. They're afraid they'll lose me—all they've put into me—they're good parents. But it's crazy; it's unnatural. I'm a grown-up man, with ideas of my own, and I'm treated as if I'm a child, a big child, but still a child."

A complicating factor in this crisis area is today's exceptionally long stretch of adolescence, which starts about age 11 or 12 and extends to 20 or 21. Teens belong to a world that emphasizes a longer childhood, a longer period of education and then a gradual entrance into the rights and responsibilities of adulthood.

For example, today the average age of marriage is 22 for females and 24 for males.

As the marriage age has risen, there has been a trend toward earlier puberty—which, in fact, is continuing downward at the rate of ten months every generation. In the 1850s, the average age of first menses was 17.5. Today, the average American girl experiences her first menstrual period at age 12.8. Ten years between puberty and marriage is a long time in a society as fast-changing, permissive and nontraditional as ours. No wonder there appears to be more sexual activity at a younger age than 100 years ago!

Consequently, the urge for independence begins earlier and lasts longer for today's teens than for their parents or grandparents.

(5) A fifth crisis area, both internal and external, is the *acceptance dilemma.* Communication often breaks down when teens and parents discuss the pros and cons of alcohol, tobacco, marijuana, pills, sniffing, sex. Honest feelings and emotions on both sides may be so strong that open, frank and reasonable discussion is impossible. Teens usually know where their parents stand on the issues and they also know where their peers

Illustrations by Melanie Statom

stand. The dilemma is: "Where am *I* going to stand?" This type of decision-making takes up considerable time and energy for both teens and parents.

CRISIS YEARS FOR PARENTS

The approaching teen years are crisis years for parents, also. In fact, George and Marie may be making more changes that produce crisis than their early adolescent children. What are some of the important changes parents go through as their children approach their teens?

(1) First of all, parents are reminded of their own *teenage experiences*. They remember the risks, the confusion—the "should I" or "shouldn't I" decisions, the agonizing mistakes. They probably remember a lot more bad than good experiences. Parents become anxious about their child going through some of the same experiences.

(2) Parents feel a *sense of loss* when they see their teen turning to friends for fun, ac-

tivity and advice. Their teen is growing into a person quite separate from the parents and letting go is hard.

(3) Parents feel upset when their *views* and *values* are *challenged*. They may long for the early years when their child accepted everything they said. "Mom and Dad are always right!" is music to parents' ears.

(4) At times parents have to *reexamine their values*. They may have taught their child values they don't fully believe in. For example, George hit the roof when Debbie brought Chico home for dinner. Yet, when Debbie was growing up, George preached equality in work, play and personal relationships.

Sometimes the values parents teach children return to them in the teen years like a boomerang. A recent family study by General Mills found that only 13 percent of parents believed that "people in authority know best." However, 69 percent wanted their *children* to believe it.

(5) Another dilemma parents have to face is that, on one hand, they feel a twinge of *jealousy* over the opportunities, choices and freedoms teens have today. Most par-

ents may remember a rather strict adolescence.

Teens confront experiences and problems that didn't exist a half generation ago. Times have changed. Parents worry a great deal about such generational differences as increased sexual activity and use of alcohol and other drugs.

What do parents think the answer is? Well, many parents believe they must *crack down hard*—in a completely different way than ever before. Sudden actions such as imposition of rigid rules and restrictions cause crises in families.

(6) Often parents are involved in *mid-life passages*. They're approaching middle age during their teen's growth years. They may be taking new steps in their personal and/or professional lives. Mom may be rejoining the work force, Dad may be changing jobs. Or Mom and Dad may be separating, ending a 15- to 20-year marriage. These changes can throw any household into chaos and confusion without the other crisis areas mentioned.

(7) Finally, a parent's *sex drive* and romantic ideas may be on a *downward cycle*, while teens are just *discovering* these drives. Such words as "puppy love" and "kid stuff" cut right to the bone when parents describe a teen's first love. Because of the opposite direction of these cycles, understanding each other may be difficult. Although teen love may be more fleeting, it is just as serious to them as their parents' love-life.

SOME SURVIVAL TACTICS

So, teen years are crisis years, not only for teens, but for their parents as well. However, most parents and teens survive the teen years, and they live happy, productive lives to old age. How do *they* do it?

If you fall into either category—teen or parent—or if you work with adolescents—you may be interested in survival tactics used successfully by those who have been through it all.

☐ Parents, *seek more information and understanding* about how teens develop. There are excellent articles, books, talks, television shows, parent education groups and classes on teen growth and development. Be on the lookout for new materials. Read all you can. Participate in programs. Talk to other, successful parents who have raised teens.

Ask these questions: "What did you do? Who helped you? What would you do again? What wouldn't you do again? How did you decide what to do?"

☐ Parents, *learn to let go*! For teens to become independent, capable adults, they can't be treated as children. Remember: "Teach them how, then let them do!" "Never do for a child what he/she can do alone."

Letting go may mean allowing your teens privacy. Leave their mail alone. Limit the length but not the content of telephone conversations. Don't look for excuses to search their room.

The more you show respect and trust, the more your teen will respect and trust you. If you established this behavior when your child was young, it will continue during teen years. However, it's never too late to start.

☐ Parents, *feel good about your authority*. You've gained valuable knowledge through your experiences. Give your teens structure and rules, but allow them some say in what those rules are going to be. A weekly family council that allows your teen to make some of the decisions that affect him or her can be helpful. Teen questionnaires show they want supervision, but they also want flexibility and understanding of individual needs and unusual situations.

☐ Parents, *examine your attitudes toward your teen*. Forget what you hear about other teens and see your child as a unique young individual (in many ways much like you). Accept your teen for and as the *person* he or she is.

☐ *Talk to your teen about sex*. Sex education begins very young and it begins in the home. Your home is a better learning place than school, church or the street. Today, many teens "fool around"; they have sex. Whether you like it or not, you must get the correct information to your child long before he or she becomes a teen. Research shows that most teens are misinformed and confused about sex and about how their body functions. One recent study found that more than 50 percent of all pregnant teenagers believed they could not get pregnant because they were too young, weren't married or didn't have intercourse very often.

☐ Teens need the *words*, *actions* and *will* to say "No." Or they need to take a realistic and responsible look at the consequences of saying "Yes." Teens need reading materials, pictures, diagrams and visual aids to understand their values, their emotions, their drives.

☐ *Try to remember some of your own teenage fears and problems*. Admitting you had questions about your own development can reassure your teen and encourage him or her to talk to you about it. Listen without always trying to get your point across. Encourage your teen to ask questions.

☐ Finally, parents, *keep your sense of humor*. If you and your teen can look at the bright side, it will help put the crises in the right perspective.

TIPS FOR TEENS

If you're a teen, some of the same survival tactics will work for you.

☐ First, *get information about the changes you are going through*. A wealth of magazine articles, pamphlets and books are available for you to gain counsel. Talk to others who have made it through adolescence. Ask them these questions: "What problems did you have with your parents?" "How did you solve them?" "Who helped you?" "What did they say? Do?" "How do you feel about the problems now?"

☐ *Ask your parents about your developing sexuality*. If they are reluctant or embarrassed to talk about it, ask for reading material, pictures, diagrams and visual aids. You *must* know how your body works.

Sometimes your parents forget that you are growing up. In fact, unconsciously, they may not want you to grow up because that means you'll eventually leave them.

☐ "Letting go" is very hard on parents. Try to understand that your parents may be going through as many changes as you are, particularly if you are the firstborn. Parents are people, too—who at times get hurt, confused, scared, uptight, irritable. *Try to see your parents' side*.

☐ *Try to figure out who you are and what you want out of life*. This search does not happen overnight; it takes a long time. Your thoughts and ideas may change often, too. But try to figure out some short- and long-range goals for yourself.

It is said that the Chinese word for *crisis* is written by combining the symbols for the words *danger* and *opportunity*. That's what's ahead—some danger and a lot of opportunity. You will need all the help you can get from your parents.

The following poem tries to catch the beauty and the tragedy that take place as a child "becomes" an adult:

> *time flies*
> *we live*
> *yesterday, today, forever*
> *time is, was*
> *is gone*
> *tender times*
> *gone forever*
>
> *time flows*
> *we feel*
> *uptight, right on*
> *out, in*
> *up, down*
> *it hurts*
> *forever*
>
> *time flees*
> *we start, stop*
> *start again*
> *develop*
> *rocking horse*
> *rock 'n roll*
> *rocking chair*
> *recycle*
>
> Shirley J. O'Brien

Building on Preadolescents' Interests

"Thirteen-year-old Sam was anxious about his slow development but, unlike another slow-growing boy, he did not take it out in mischievous show-off techniques; his teacher allowed him to apply his math in making detailed blueprints for a boat, which his Shop teacher then helped him to build. Twelve-year-old Sally was precociously adolescent; her 'Home Ec' teacher helped her to design and make some teenage clothes and in addition helped her experiment with new hairdos. In these and many other instances teachers who understand the new drive pressures, ambitions, hopes and anxieties of children this age can provide constructive outlets for their tensions and help to sustain their confidence and positive self-image.

"The most successful teachers . . . maintain good structure, partly by making demands and providing opportunities which build on children's interests and which bring achievement that seems worthwhile and thus supports the shaky self-confidence of children this age. These successful teachers are understanding when the children are restless but help them to harness their energies in activities; they don't allow the group experience to become chaotic, but they do not become sadistic in maintaining control because their control is built on the children's own wish for achievement. These teachers avoid boring, repetitious, monotonous assignments at the stage when children find it hard to pay attention to routine tasks; they look for challenging, relevant work that utilizes children's interests."—LOIS BARCLAY MURPHY, "Enjoying Preadolescence: The Forgotten Years," in *Early Adolescents: Understanding and Nurturing Their Development* (Washington, DC: ACEI, 1978).

Redefining the Child Care "Problem"— Men as Child Nurturers

James A. Levine

ABOUT A YEAR AND A HALF AGO, I unexpectedly found myself in the middle of a fascinating discussion. The occasion was a cocktail party for faculty and members of the Board of Trustees of a large women's college. I had just started sipping on my gin and tonic and was busily trying to locate the peanuts when a trustee who is a senior partner in a prominent law firm in Boston started telling me about his *problem* with women attorneys.

But before specifying the problem, he gave me some background, laid out the record—as lawyers will do—point by point. Number one: he was an absolute supporter of equal rights and opportunities for women. Number two: he had been a pioneer in the legal community in the hiring of women. And number three: he was, after all, a trustee of this college (which, again, is a women's school).

The problem was this: he'd hire these bright female attorneys and after a few years, just after they got to know the ropes, just after they'd served their apprenticeship and could start earning some money for the firm, they got pregnant and wanted to take a leave of absence.

It was making things quite difficult for him, and he was obviously quite perturbed. Looking at me with a pitch for sympathy— *man to man*—he said, "What are *we* going to do about this state of affairs?"

I don't think he really expected me to have a solution, much less to redefine the problem. So he was somewhat surprised when, instead of shrugging my shoulders, I asked him if his firm happened to employ men as well as women.

"Of course it does," he said.

I asked if any of those men ever became fathers during their tenure at his firm.

"Of course they do," he said.

"Well, then," I said, "the solution is at hand."

I suggested that he implement a paternity leave policy at his firm. More than that, I

43

suggested that he *encourage* its use by male employees. It was not a short-term solution, I said, but one which—if pursued vigorously—would ultimately cause his *problem* with female attorneys to disappear. Requests for maternity leave would continue, of course, but they would no longer seem anomalous. They would just be a part of the new rhythm of work, promoted by his policy of *parental* leave. His long record as a progressive employer would, of course, continue. It might even be embellished if he thought about subsidizing a day care program for the children of mothers *and* fathers in his firm. Knowing that they had a secure place for their children, his employees might take shorter leaves of absence.

Just then his wife said, "You know, dear, maybe he's got something there."

But I don't think he heard her. His head was shaking back and forth as he made his way to the bar for a refill. I don't think I solved his problem.

About "Making Babies"

Of course it was not just *his* problem, that babies require time and care and energy. In fact, that very evening, when I came home from the cocktail party, I came across a guest column in *Newsweek* which some of you may have seen. The column was entitled "Making Babies," and it was written by a twenty-five-year-old woman, Anne Taylor Fleming, then four years out of Sarah Lawrence College. A note at the bottom of the page indicated that Ms. Fleming and her husband, Karl, were a "writing team" and that they had spent the last year and a half researching and co-authoring a book.

In her essay, Ms. Fleming shared the agony and conflict she felt as she con-templated motherhood. The most compelling reason she gave for herself, and for others of her generation, for not wanting to get pregnant was—and I'm quoting—"I have a career to pursue and I can't risk dividing my energies and loyalties between work and a baby."

It was a poignant statement, not only for what it said but for what it left out. For as she looked to the future, Ms. Fleming nowhere mentioned her writing partner, her husband Karl. Nowhere did she mention that motherhood for her would mean fatherhood for Karl, that his presence could or would in any way reduce the conflict between career and childrearing, or that there might in fact be a sharing of joy in the sharing of parenthood. They had just spent a year and a half making a book together; but making a baby and caring for it was her project, and hers alone.

MORE ABOUT MEN AND CHILDREARING

It is not surprising, really, that either Anne Taylor Fleming or our trustee-attorney don't think about fathers when they think about childrearing, that they don't think about how having a career and having a family might bear on the lives of men. Not only are we socialized toward thinking of childrearing as a woman's activity; we're socialized *against* thinking of it as an appropriate male function, let alone one that could form a major component of male identity.

Often the argument is that this separation of functions is *for the good of the children*, as in this example from Dr. Haim Ginott's *Between Parent and Child* (1965), a guidebook on parenting which is a standard text

James A. Levine is Research Fellow, Center for Research on Women in Higher Education and the Professions, Wellesley College, Wellesley, Massachusetts. He recently received the 14th Family Life Book Award from the Child Study Association of America for his book, Who Will Raise the Children? New Options for Fathers (and Mothers) (New York: Lippincott, 1976; see review on p. 33 of October 1977 CE).

in high school and college courses on family life and parent education and which sits on the living room shelf in millions of American households. Dr. Ginott warns us—and I am quoting:[1]

In the modern family . . . many men find themselves involved in mothering activities, such as feeding, diapering, and bathing a baby. Though some men welcome these new opportunities for closer contact with their infants, there is the danger that the baby may end up with two mothers, rather than with a mother and a father.

Not, significantly, the possibility that the baby might end up with two *parents*!

Legal Locksteps

Like Dr. Ginott, courts of law and the legal profession are wont to think it dangerous for men to get too involved in childrearing. Consider, if you will, that, as recently as 1971, a standard handbook on family law written for practicing attorneys in Minnesota (Rorris 1971) said:[2]

Except in very rare cases, the father should not have the custody of the minor children of the parties. He is usually unqualified psychologically and emotionally; nor does he have the time and care to supervise the children. A lawyer not only does an injustice to himself, but he is unfair to his client, to the state, and to society if he gives any encouragement to the father that he should have custody of his children. A lawyer who encourages his client to file for custody, unless it is one of the classic exceptions, has difficulty collecting his fee, has a most unreasonable client, has taken the time of the court and the welfare agencies involved, and has put a burden on his legal brethren.

Perhaps that seems to you an extreme case. But I would suggest that the attitudes of many in the legal profession and of Dr.

[1] *Editor's note:* Dr. Alice Ginott, widow of Dr. Ginott, informs us that before his death he stated his desire to change this paragraph so as to emphasize that fathers are indeed very important to children.

[2] Happily, this publication has been withdrawn from use in Minnesota since 1972.

Ginott are deeply ingrained, albeit in more subtle ways, in our society.

Missing Statistics

Consider, for example, that even as the government monitors changes in family structure it maintains and perpetuates a very limited and biased perception of parental roles. The Department of Labor recently told us that some 37 percent of preschool children and slightly over 50 percent of school-aged children have working mothers. Nowhere are the statistics to be found on children of working fathers. We keep tabs on working mothers because they, and not working fathers, pose a social dilemma: after all, if women work, who will take care of the children? ("Working mothers" signals an inherent conflict of commitment; "working fathers" is a redundancy.)

Often the answer is day care, the area to which I devote most of my working time. But even here, the tendency is to reinforce the notion that the care of children is or should be relevant only to the lives of women. In a speech about day care, the distinguished psychologist Uri Bronfenbrenner (1975), who is an impassioned advocate of national policies supportive of family life, had this to say (and I think his comments are not atypical of most national leaders):

I think that day care should include a guiding principle, one of allowing the *mother* a freedom of choice so that *she* is not forced either to provide no care for *her* children or, in effect, forced to leave the child in a situation which *she* does not regard as acceptable.

No consideration here that it would be easier for her to deal with the children if experts and government agencies did not keep insisting that the children are hers and hers alone.

I could go on citing example after example to show you how deep and in some instances how bizarre is the resistance to the notion of men as childrearers. I could tell you, for example, about a study, done in 1971, of "Father Participation in Infancy," which had a curious research design: as the researchers admitted sheepishly in a·footnote, they never got around to interviewing, much less observing, any fathers. All of their results were based on talks with mothers.

Every reader of CHILDHOOD EDUCATION could, I am sure, share similar stories with me.

A "Woman's Problem"?

Suffice it to say that, after all the stories are added up, the matter of child care, the conflict between work and family life, persists—understood both publicly and privately as a *woman's* problem. And so, in their private lives women like Anne Taylor Fleming increasingly feel that the risk of parenthood is indeed too great. In the corporate world, those like our trustee-attorney, feeling stung by the affirmative action plans they supported, shrug their shoulders and say, "What are we going to do about this state of affairs?"

What we are going to do, I would suggest, will never be enough—at either the interpersonal or the broader social level—unless we begin redefining the problem, unless we begin looking at the law firm or the factory as a place that employs *both* working mothers and working fathers, at the family as a place where *two* working parents can share in the opportunity and responsibility offered in caring for their children, and at day care as a service that can and does support both men and women.

LESSONS FROM SCANDINAVIA

But is it really possible to redefine the problem? Examples from two Scandinavian countries will perhaps indicate to you just what I mean by redefinition.

Norway's Families of the Future

For the last several years the Family Council in Norway—a government agency which has no analogue in the United States—has been attempting to design a social program responsive to the needs of what it calls "the family of the future," the family with young children and two working parents. Why they call it the "family of the future" I'm not quite sure, since in Norway—as in the United States—such families are already prevalent, fast becoming the majority. But the point is, the Norwegians are actively trying to develop supports for these families—and by supports they don't mean just day care for "working mothers." They are, indeed, developing more day care and preschool programs; but they are also saying that day care outside the home is only a partial solution to the stresses on parents with young children. The full solution has to give parents external support *and* allow and encourage them to share more in childrearing. And so the Norwegians have implemented a "work-sharing experiment" in which both parents work outside the home, but neither less than 16 nor more than 28 hours per week. The experiment is small, but it involves employees at all levels—from the assembly line on up through management— and in a variety of occupations. Although not a mandatory program, it has been very popular; employers have found that their productivity does not suffer, and both mothers and fathers have found that the slight sacrifice in income is more than compensated for by feeling that they can cope— that they are not overwhelmed with work and parenthood, that they can share, that they can have time for their children and for one another.

Sweden's Parental Insurance

Sweden, too, has been thinking about the family of the future, and starting to do something about it in the present. In the mid-sixties the Swedes realized that what they had been calling the "women's problem" was but one half of a much broader "sex-role problem" that included both men and women. It was not enough to advocate more day nurseries for children of working mothers, for men too were parents, and men too were constrained by their socially conditioned sex roles. As Swedish Prime Minister Olof Palme said in an address to the United Nations, "The greatest disadvantage with the male sex role is that the man has too small a share in the upbringing of the children."

And so, like the Norwegians, the Swedes have started implementing policies to encourage men to participate actively in child-rearing. The most notable is the policy of parental insurance, which allows either parent to stay home for a period of seven months after the birth of a baby and still receive 90 percent of pre-birth salary. The mother can stay home for three months and the father for four, or vice versa; or they can each work part-time for seven months. The kicker is that if the man does stay home, the family is entitled to an extra month of parental insurance.

BACK TO THE USA: RESTRUCTURING WORK

I do not mean to suggest, in raising these examples, that foreign social experiments are readily transplantable in American soil. Nor am I sanguine about the speed or ease with which the sort of redefinition I am talking about can occur. A great amount of resistance and anxiety is involved—at the personal and institutional levels—in any sort of change, not to mention one that involves the very structure of work and our traditional definitions of male and female roles.

We do not have, as some of the Scandinavian countries do, any cohesive national policy for families and children. President Carter has talked about developing a family policy and the White House is planning to hold a major conference on the family in 1979,[3] at which time some of the issues I am talking about may come to the fore. In the meantime, however, an increase can be noted in the scattering of efforts around the country to redefine the child care problem— and its solution—by restructuring work.

Job-Sharing

In Los Angeles, a middle management executive with a major national corporation recently told his boss that he wanted to cut down his work from five days to three so that he could be at home more with his six-month-old baby. When the company tried out the idea, albeit cautiously, it found that business did not come to a halt *and* it reaped an unexpected benefit when it faced a financial setback. With the example of their part-time male executive in mind, the company refrained from sending out routine letters of

[3]*Editor's note:* Three conferences were held in 1980 in Baltimore, Minneapolis and Los Angeles.

dismissal. Instead, it sent around a memo asking if anybody else wanted to work part-time. Lo and behold, there were many people—men and women—who wanted a part-time option but who had been afraid to ask, afraid that their commitment to work would be questioned. They were not all mothers and fathers; some wanted time to go to school or to pursue hobbies. The point is, once more flexibility was built into the system, sanctioned by the system, people took advantage of it.

Up the California coast, in San Francisco, a firm called New Ways To Work is very actively trying to build-in such flexibility by promoting the concept of "job-sharing." As the name implies, job-sharing means that two people work at one job. New Ways To Work teaches pairs of individuals how to apply for jobs that have been advertised for one person, and it teaches employers how to redesign jobs so that they can be shared by two people. As a result of its efforts, New Ways To Work has people working in shared jobs in nine school systems, in city planning departments, in top-level hospital administrative posts, and in many, many other positions that would seem to resist restructuring.

Flextime

As much as I love California (I lived there for four years and often dream of it, especially during the winter), I don't mean to suggest that it is the only place where change is taking place. Throughout the country, one of the fastest growing innovations in work restructuring—and one that has enormous implications for child care—is flextime. In flextime scheduling, workers usually put in a "core" shift of hours, such as 9 a.m. to 3

p.m., but can adjust their arrival or departure according to their personal needs. They might, for example, arrive at 7 a.m. and leave at 3 p.m.; or they might arrive at 8 a.m. and leave at 4 p.m.; and so on. In some cases, extra hours worked one week can be carried over to the next. Flextime is usually proposed as a way of increasing worker satisfaction (which it does), decreasing traffic congestion (which it does), and allowing women to reconcile work and family obligations. It does that too—mothers can see their kids off to school or day care or can be home with them after school—but, I want to add, it works just as well for men too!

A Step at a Time

But, you may ask, what does this all add up to? A little bit of change here, a bit more there. As I said before, change is slow and difficult. I would not discount the importance of small steps along the way that make it more possible for us to accept change on a larger scale. Nor would I discount the importance of federal legislation which, if passed, would give this country its first major experiment in job restructuring, mandating that 10 percent of all federal jobs be available on a permanent part-time, flextime, or shared basis. And I mean jobs up to the level of GS-18, which is about $40,000 per year.

I have been focusing my remarks on work restructuring not to suggest that it is practical, feasible or desirable for everybody to work part-time or flextime, but to suggest that in the United States, as in the Scandinavian countries, redefining the child care problem will mean looking seriously at the work that men and women do, because the structure of work has an enormous hold on our lives.

SUPPORTING BOTH MEN
AND WOMEN

Nor do I mean to suggest that changes in work structure will adequately redefine the problem, that they will break down deeply held attitudinal resistances (shared by men and women) to fuller participation by men in childrearing.

Redefining the child care problem means working in all sectors of our society to break down sex-role stereotypes, and to broaden our vision of nurturance as a quality that is fundamentally human, not male or female.

It means, for example, not only implementing nonsexist curricula in the early childhood setting (and all other educational settings), but filling out such curricula to let children know not only that women can be police officers and letter carriers and construction workers, but that men can be nursery school teachers and elementary teachers and nurses and that—yes—daddies can do more than go off to work. (If any of you work in early childhood settings I'm sure you can attest to the scarcity of any materials that show men in nurturing roles.)

Redefining the child care problem means opening up opportunities within the school systems so that older children can be rewarded or valued in caring for younger children. That doesn't mean broad complicated social changes; it means opening up opportunities for cross-age helping within our local elementary schools and arranging field work credit so that high school boys (and girls) can work in local day care and nursery programs.

It means changing hospital policies that exclude men from the delivery room or, as almost happened to me, allow men into the delivery room but then relegate them to the status of non-parents by letting them visit their newborns from 7-7:30 p.m.

It means taking a whole new view of the male life cycle, of creating a life-space, when children are young, for men to receive psychological and social support, as women have, if they want to temporarily reduce their commitment to work outside the home.

And yes, it does mean implementing the paternity leave policies—as several American cities already have done—that so boggled the mind of the trustee-attorney from that women's college.

The answers we are seeking in trying to work out lives that offer us equal opportunity, that allow us to be productive and to be loving and caring for our children, won't come easy. But in the long run, they may not come at all if we keep defining child care as a "woman's problem" or if we think of day care as a social mechanism to "accommodate" the "changing role of women." The question before us as individuals and as a nation beginning to think about developing a "family policy" is, "How can we support both men and women in working out new options for work and family life?" It is a question that is broader, more difficult, and ultimately, I think, more rewarding for us all.

References

Bronfenbrenner, Urie. "Public Policy and the Survival of Families." *Voice for Children* 8, 4 (Apr. 1975): 2. Reprinted by permission of author and publisher (Washington, DC: Day Care and Child Development Council of America, Inc.).

Ginott, Haim G. *Between Parent and Child.* New York: Macmillan, 1965. Reprinted by permission.

Rorris, James P. "Separation Agreements—Support for the Spouse and Minor Children." *Minnesota Family Law, Minnesota Practice Manual* 50. St. Paul, MN: Continuing Legal Education. Issued by University of Minnesota, 1971. P. 75. Reprinted by permission of Continuing Legal Education.

Improving the Quality of Family Life

Dorothy W. Gross

IS THE AMERICAN FAMILY at risk? Is it no longer able to meet the needs of children for nurturance and socialization and of parents for emotional connection and a sense of continuity? If so, shall we say good riddance to a bankrupt institution—or mourn the loss of a valuable one? On both sides of the issue may be found respected scholars and contributors to the mass literature alike. Those who point with alarm to the crumbling of the family vie with those who welcome a wide array of experimental or variant forms. All the analysts, however, concur in the view that the American family has undergone rapid and radical change in the past thirty years. *What are the facts? What do they suggest for children? What are the implications for educators and schools?*

DATA SPEAK

First, the evidence. We find clear documentation of a decrease in family size. This change is due only partly to the widely recognized lower birth rate. Equally significant is the decreased number of adults in the home due to divorce, unmarried parenthood, and the virtual disappearance of home-based

"Despite the stated doubts of many parents that the schools are doing their job, when children are having special problems the preferred source of help for most parents is teachers and principals. Is this a contradiction? I don't think so."

Dorothy W. Gross is a member of the Faculty, Graduate Programs, Bank Street College of Education, New York City.

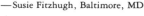
—Susie Fitzhugh, Baltimore, MD

in-laws, lodgers and servants. One out of every six children under 18 is living in a single-parent home, with the rate increasing most rapidly for children under 6. The largest category of single parenthood involves divorced women, followed closely by women under 25 who never married.

Another factor in family change is the increased incidence of working mothers. The majority of married mothers of school-age children now work, two-thirds of them full-time. One-third of married mothers with children under 6 are working, three times as many as thirty years ago. The rates are higher still in families without both parents present. In single-parent families, almost three-quarters of those with school-age children and over half with children under 6 are working, 80 percent full-time.

A third factor is the sharply rising birth rate among teenagers. Currently, one of every ten adolescent girls gives birth to a baby before reaching the age of 18. The national statistics reveal a litany of conditions significantly correlated with teenage parenthood, among them child abuse, prematurity with its associated handicaps, unemployment, and a high rate of divorce.

51

LIMITED ADULT SUPPORT

What is revealed by these data is a very large—and growing—number of children with limited access to adults. Parents are working and, if very young, are burdened with their own unsatisfied needs. A tragic indicator of their frustrations is the rising number of reported child-abuse cases. The care of children too often tends to be divided among busy parents, equally busy neighbors, often inadequate day care centers, television sets and the street. Satisfaction of even basic health care is often neglected. It is recognized that 20 million children do not receive primary care, complete immunizations, and/or prompt and early treatment of disease. Other needs—for support, instruction and models for identification—increasingly are sought in peer groups. These, commonly unstable both in their composition and their judgment, offer little of the comfort and real help that children need. As a consequence, peer-oriented children often develop premature coping skills designed for adjustment and survival, but not founded on genuine trust and a sense of security. The individualism of American society is notable in parents' increasing emphasis on their own self-actualization and lessened willingness to sacrifice for their children.

CONFUSION ABOUT CHILD CARE

Even in homes where parents are present, there is much confusion about childrearing values and, indeed, about personal beliefs. The General Mills American Family Report (Yankelovich, Skelly and White 1977) revealed parents worried about being too permissive and about expecting too much from their children. They worry about television violence while themselves using spanking and yelling as disciplinary measures. They believe in egalitarian ways of raising boys and girls while themselves enacting traditional roles. They disapprove of their older children eating junk food between meals and not doing family chores. They are upset about their younger children's whining and temper tantrums. They want access to study groups about drugs and smoking, classroom teaching methods, children's nutrition and medical problems, discipline and sex and the problems of parenting. At the same time, they tend to be reluctant to seek out advice, particularly from juvenile authorities, family agencies, social workers and health clinics.

Nevertheless, despite the stated doubts of many parents that the schools are doing their job, when children are having special problems the preferred source of help for most parents is teachers and school principals. Is this a contradiction? I don't think so. Rather, I see it as a recognition of the stability and familiarity of the school and, perhaps, its potential, however imperfectly realized, as a helping institution. Teachers are prototypes of parents, once removed, evoking feelings of dependency, devotion and, not uncommonly, expectations of authority and expertise. It would not require a major shift in perception for parents to view teachers and other school personnel as important resources for family needs. The changes required would be in schools.

Too often the school as an institution has become a self-perpetuating system. Its formal goal of education is transformed into the goals of institutional preservation and the maintenance of order. It becomes increasingly removed from the real needs of the children it purportedly serves and loses the support of its community. A poignant indicator of this loss of support is the widespread voting-down of school bond issues by citizens who do not see the salience of schooling for their children's lives.

How then can schools reshape themselves to meet the new needs of children and families?

SCHOOLS AS FAMILIES

Rising numbers of children are growing up in small families with limited access to adult support. The increasing divorce rate is exposing children to the emotional stress of separation from a parent. An increasing number of children are growing up with teenage mothers whose own unmet needs and lack of education lead to child abuse and poverty and poor health. Large numbers of children must rely on each other for comfort and care, since many parents are confused about child-rearing values and changing sex roles. *The challenge to the school is to broaden its traditional area of service and to become an extended family.* It is no longer enough to focus narrowly on cognitive skills, if ever it was. "Back to basics" as a slogan is not nearly basic enough: a truly basic approach to education involves the recognition of the wholeness of a child's being in the context of his family and community. Health, adequate nutrition and sleep, economic security, safe and comfortable living quarters, emotional ease are surely not irrelevant to learn-

ing. Why, then, can schools not become centers for total family development?

Day care centers, Head Start programs and nursery schools have long considered their function a comprehensive one. What is proposed here is that all schools might adopt a family model, particularly since so many children and parents have multiple unmet needs and limited resources for fulfillment of these. How would it work?

Each elementary school building—or each pair or trio of buildings—would include a range of programs:

- [ ] indoor and outdoor education and recreation for children from infancy through the middle years
- [ ] early morning and late afternoon day care
- [ ] adult classes and recreational activities
- [ ] tutoring and homework help for children
- [ ] a crafts center where parents and teachers might create learning materials for children
- [ ] discussion and support groups for parents
- [ ] a health and nutrition center for children to receive basic examinations and inoculations and for parents to have access to health resources
- [ ] a center for psychological services, including an evening and weekend emergency "hot line"
- [ ] special supports and classes for pregnant girls, adolescent parents, and young families
- [ ] availability of breakfast and lunch
- [ ] a swap center for outgrown clothing
- [ ] opportunities for community volunteers to teach and demonstrate a variety of skills
- [ ] summer activities for families.

Space for these expanded functions would be available in many communities where the reduced birth rate has resulted in empty school buildings. In others, existing space would have to be redesigned to meet a variety of needs. A changed time frame is also called for: families do not fit their lives into 8:40-3:00 slots. Services and resources must be available early mornings, evenings, weekends, summers.

NEW TEACHERS FOR NEW NEEDS

But most important is the need for educators who can function broadly, not only as teachers of facts and skills but as assessors of development. If schools are to be comprehensive centers of family development, practitioners need to recognize the ways in which their disciplines overlap. Teachers specialize in learning and cognition, nurses in health, psychologists in mental health, and social workers in community life—but all are involved with the totality of a person as he or she copes with the challenges of life. A person's totality is not divided into neat segments labeled "body," "mind" or "psyche." We perceive and interpret experience with our whole selves. For example, malnutrition or grief influences children's ability to learn as surely as the quality of their thinking shapes their self-image. And family life affects individual development even as individuals create families. This complexity of transaction requires educators to add psychosocial knowledge and skills to their more traditional expertise in curriculum and teaching. They need to develop sensitivity to feelings, skills of listening and of observing nonverbal behavior, knowledge of family dynamics and child development, information about human services, ability to make referrals. Such areas of knowledge and skill can no longer be limited to the province of psychological experts, since there can never be enough of these and the teacher is the front-line contact person for most children and parents.

Until major institutional change does take place in our schools, teachers and administrators can begin shifting some of their priorities now—that is, facilitating change by embodying it. Less time can be spent on testing and grading children and more on listening to them. Less time can be spent on formal reports to parents and more on genuinely communicative conferences. Families can be encouraged to visit the school informally: space can be found for an easy chair or two, a coffee pot, a playpen or a piece of carpeting for the baby. Mutual support groups may emerge spontaneously if given a chance. A local health center or clinic might be interested in an outpost in the school. Nutritious snacks can be available. Volunteers, particularly grandparents, can be invited to teach or visit. A clothing center can be started. Curriculum can reflect current realities: children can tell and write and draw their experiences and feelings and teachers can bring materials—pictures, books, films, personal stories—that show understanding of the griefs and problems of childhood. Many of these simple ideas are already being enacted in many schools.

Finding ways to meet real needs is not so difficult once we face the existence of those needs. The real challenge is the reshaping of traditional ways of behaving. If the American family is changing, can we do less than to change the American school?

Bibliography

Graubard, Stephen R., ed. "The Family." *Daedalus* 106, 2 (Spring 1977). Journal of the American Academy of Arts and Sciences.

National Academy of Sciences. *Toward a National Policy for Children and Families.* Washington, DC: The Academy, 1976.

Yankelovich, Skelly & White, Inc. *Raising Children in a Changing Society.* The General Mills American Family Report 1976-77. Minneapolis, MN: General Mills, Inc., 1977.

Establishing a Parent Education Resource Center

Patricia Edmister

"Please, Mommy, let's take this fire truck home today," says one child. "I want a puzzle and a record!" says another.

"I know you want to stay longer and look at the children's book, Susie, but we just *have* to get home before Tommy's school is out," a mother pleads.

Another mother: "There are so many books to choose from—it's fantastic! I'll just have to keep coming back until I've read them all!"

These are but a few comments overheard one morning at the Parent Education Resource Center in Montgomery County, Maryland. Parents and young children have found the Center to be a great new place to spend time together in a setting they find to be both fun and informative. The children especially enjoy the opportunity to choose toys, books and records, which they can use at the Center and also can check out for use at home. Parents enjoy a library facility full of materials about parenting, with a children's area right there where they can keep a close watch on the child's activities and not have to worry about safety or noise annoying other library patrons. Many of the families come as a carpool, making a social occasion of the trip.

Need for a Resource Center

Until recently, relatively little emphasis has been given by the U.S. federal government to the importance of parent education. Rather, parenting skills were assumed to be something that "came naturally" when a child arrived. But the 1970 White House Conference on Children and Youth alerted American educators to the necessity of ex-panding programs to help families improve their childrearing practices. In the past, parents seeking information regarding parenting skills sought support and experiential information from grandparents and other members of the extended family. Today's mobility makes it increasingly difficult for members of the nuclear family to avail themselves of these traditional resources; consequently, the primary responsibility for developing happy, healthy children falls on parents with few support systems to aid them. They are therefore seeking information and guidance from a variety of places and people—books, magazines, television shows, friends and parent groups. In Montgomery County, Maryland, an affluent suburban area bordering Washington, D.C., parent education classes with a life-cycle approach offered through the Department of Adult Education, Montgomery County Public Schools, are proving a significant source of information and support for parents.*

As a consequence of the increasing requests for materials related to parenting, local libraries in Montgomery County have been unable to keep sufficient numbers of books available to meet demand. Many resources such as movies, tapes, film-strip/record presentations, as well as professional journals and periodicals of interest to professional parent-educators and parents, have been especially difficult to obtain. Thus, our Adult Education Department has established a Parent Education Resource Center in a centrally located junior high school, to provide service and materials to those desiring extensive information.

Back by popular demand, with more concrete ways to help parents become effective educators of their children, is Patricia Edmister, Parent Education Specialist, Department of Adult Education, Montgomery County Public Schools, Rockville, Maryland.

Population Served

This facility is open to the public from 9:00 to 4:00 daily. We encourage parents to bring their young children with them, so that the latter may play in the carpeted children's area which is provided with toys, books and a discovery corner for children's use. Visits to the Center by special groups such as Head Start parents, Title I parents, foster parents, day care mothers, and university classes are also welcomed—for, once people visit the Center, they frequently return on their own (see Table 1).

In addition, we ask our parent educators with the Department of Adult Education to take resource materials to their classes for distribution to parents who are unable to come to the Center. Thus, materials are distributed to more individuals than appear on the attendance summaries below.

Physical Facilities

To establish our Center we converted a traditional junior high school classroom into a library-type facility, with one corner carpeted and semi-enclosed by low, three-shelf bookcases holding a variety of children's toys to be played with on-site. Located here too are numerous children's books, chosen with consultative help from the county library service. A children's discovery corner, with child-sized and sturdy furniture, has been designed to stimulate children's curiosity with activities of interest to preschoolers and materials that are easily manipulated and explored.

The adult area, lined with bookshelves and display stands filled with current publications of interest to parents, also includes a number of tables and chairs, offering parents, professionals and students an opportun-

Table 1

| | Total Attendance | | Books Circulated | | | | Audiovisual | | New Patrons | |
	Adults	Children	Adult	Children	Records	Toys	Materials	Pamphlets	Adults	Children
RESOURCE CENTER ATTENDANCE AND CIRCULATION October 1976–May 1977										
October	124	44	160	42	33	43	5	Not recorded	Not recorded	
November (19 days)	155	121	157	97	77	104	6	Not recorded	Not recorded	
December (21 days)	126	115	119	112	69	91	2	Not recorded	17	6
January (18.5 days)	120	95	163	103	54	91	8	Not recorded	32	9
February (16 days)	214	167	256	159	121	86	10	41	82	67
March (22 days)	270	213	332	191	143	101	4	23	68	60
April (10 days)	211	101	153	94	71	69	2	49	56	17
May (19 days)	163	112	185	94	61	64	10	51	35	15
Eight-month total	1,383	968	1,525	892	629	649	47	164	290	174

ity to peruse information at their leisure or do research in an ideal academic atmosphere. Tables can be arranged to accommodate group meetings. To acquaint groups interested in parent education with the resources available, we invite them to use this space. A third area provides multimedia audiovisual equipment for use in viewing and listening to the various filmstrip/record programs on parenting, previewing slide presentations, listening to children's records (equipped with earphones to avoid disturbing others in attendance), or viewing videotape cassettes.

The fourth area houses the record and toy lending facility and the librarian's desk, where materials are lent and returned.

Equipment Requirements

Equipment requirements for a resource center will vary, depending on availability of resources within the location. Because our Center is located within a public school, we have a film projector and screen handy when needed. Filmstrip and slide projectors would also be shared by most schools, although we purchased some for our Center so that they can be borrowed by parent-educators for use in their classes. Additional equipment purchased included:

    2 cassette tape recorders and tapes
    1 typewriter
    1 record player
    Secretarial desk and chair
    Four-drawer file
    Library tables
    Filmstrip and record machine
    Card catalog cabinet
    Children's book and record browser
    Display stands
    Slide previewer
    Slide projector

Frequently schools and businesses have surplus equipment they are willing to donate to organizations such as ours for tax deductions.

Lending Policies

We allow all printed materials (with the exception of professional journals), records and toys to be borrowed for two weeks, with a limit of two books and two records per adult and two books per child. One toy per child may also be borrowed, with a family limit of three toys.

A professional individual (defined as a teacher, an educator, an agency representative working in the Washington Metropolitan area) may make special arrangements, according to availability and need. Audiovisual aids, available to professionals or parent groups by such special arrangements, may be used for one week. We charge fines of five cents per day for overdue adult materials and two cents per day for children's materials.

Materials

Our Center makes a variety of materials available for both adults and children. The adult materials are shelved according to categories such as: Pregnancy and Birth, Infant and Child Development, Child Health and Child Care, Special Children Parenting, Fathers, Intellectual Development, Play, Activities for Children, Teacher Aids, Child Development Textbooks. Periodicals and professional journals are also on hand for reference (we have ordered two subscriptions each of a number of selected titles).

Through the government printing offices we obtain many pamphlets and paperback materials at nominal cost, and many other

materials are provided free from State and Local Extension Services and Departments of Public Health. Maintaining close contact with agencies in the community has proved of considerable help in outfitting the Center with materials as well as equipment; accordingly we set aside a table for flyers, announcements, items of public interest, information about meetings or programs available throughout the community. A con-

veniently placed community bulletin board highlights items of interest to parents and notes from persons seeking other parents and children to form play groups. In addition, the Center maintains a vertical file of articles of interest or single-copy pamphlets for reference.

Toy Lending

A toy lending facility can help parents provide intellectual stimulation for their chil-

dren by making available a variety of toys and by offering seminars to help parents learn to use these toys to stimulate their children. Our toy lending library includes a multitude of toys designed for different interests and age levels. Push-pull toys, puzzles, educational games, cars and trucks, musical instruments, threading beads, and pegboards are a few of the items we make available. In addition to the toys for loan, we maintain the on-site, carpeted play area with large motor manipulative materials, a standing mirror, child-size chairs and tables and beanbag chairs for children to lounge in while perusing the children's books located there. We hold two-hour Toy-Play workshops for parents prior to their obtaining a borrower's card, to give information on the importance of play for developing motor coordination, positive self-concept, and language skills.

Records

Also available for loan is an assortment of long-playing children's records, including music of rhythm bands, folk songs, activity games, nursery rhymes, and favorite children's stories and holiday music.

Audiovisual Materials

As previously noted, several sound-filmstrips and films applicable to early childhood parent education can be borrowed through the Center; but due to cost of films, most are ordered through the public school or county library systems.

Occasionally we schedule film days, with showing of appropriate films for young children and others on normal growth and development for parents.

Personnel Requirements

Our Center has managed to function with the services of one part-time (30 hours per week) librarian who is needed for checking materials in and out, processing new books and materials, maintaining materials in the center, typing correspondence and notices, and performing general receptionist functions.

Extension of Services

Although our Resource Center is geographically located mid-county, many people are still unable to visit it. Consequently, we encourage parent education instructors throughout the county to take materials out to classes for subsequent distribution. A mobile van, able to move around the county, would be an advantage for highly rural or geographically large districts; but we have not been able to afford such a service through our Resource Center at the present time.

Sum-up

Research in early childhood education has demonstrated repeatedly the positive effects of parent-child interaction. Today, a major area of emphasis in childhood education is parent education. But for parents to become effective educators of their children, classes and resources must be readily available to them. Response to Montgomery County's (Maryland) Parent Education Resource Center has been excellent. Perhaps you, too, will find this an effective way to help parents.

* For a comprehensive overview of the entire Parent Education Life-Cycle Approach, see the January 1977 issue of CHILDHOOD EDUCATION (pp. 122-27).

Working with Parents on the Run

Shari Nedler

IN A REVIEW of the effectiveness of early intervention programs, Urie Bronfenbrenner (1974) concludes that actively involving families of children enrolled in early childhood education programs is critical to a program's success. He further suggests that parents not only reinforce the effects of the program while it is operational but also contribute to sustaining positive effects after it ends. More and more evidence (Gordon, 1971; Levenstein, 1970; Klaus and Gray, 1968; Gilmer et al., 1970; Karnes et al., 1969) has been reported to support the importance of involving parents in the education of their young children.

Some commonly used strategies for parental involvement include: group meetings at school, home visits, home-based approaches such as Home Start or Levenstein's toy-demonstrator program, and the establishment of Parent Child Centers. Each of these approaches assumes that parents are accessible and able to commit the time necessary for acquiring new skills relevant to effective child rearing.

Some Real Life Problems

While few of us might argue seriously with the importance of parental involvement, we all know that many problems exist regarding the actual commitment of time for this purpose. Many parents work, and their only contact with the preschool or day care staff occurs when they drop their children off in the morning or pick them up at night. To compound this problem, a large number of these working parents are divorced, widowed or single. Forced to cope with raising their children alone, they may be barely subsisting at the poverty level.

Many center programs, anxious to provide services to parents, face funding limitations which seem to prohibit offering any ancillary services. Additional constraints often include available staff-time and access to special expertise.

Despite these problems, options do exist that would permit varying levels of involvement for all parents. Rather than giving up and limiting goals, we may not yet have explored all alternatives. One especially worthy of examination is working with parents "on the run."

Basic Assumptions

Assuming that some or all of the constraints described above will be present in most program settings, the staff must select and order priorities. Once committed to the idea that parent involvement and education are impor-

*Many parents who work outside the home still want
to be involved in the education of their young children.
Here are a host of practical ways you can help!*

*Shari Nedler is Coordinator of the Early Childhood Program,
University of Colorado at Denver.*

Photo courtesy of Parent & Infant Development Program, Dept. of Adult Ed., Montgomery Co., MD, Public Schools

tant and can make a difference, they need to accept as realistic facts limitations of funds, staff-time, parent-time and even lack of parent interest. Turning these factors around so that they emerge as positive forces must become a major goal. It can be done! The "on the run" approach to be described herein is based on certain assumptions:

Assumption 1: Although funds may be limited, or even nonexistent, activities can be developed using materials found around the home, resources from the community, or toys made by parents and volunteers. Babies and toddlers constantly learn from their natural environment; expensive educational toys are therefore not at all essential to the learning process. Creative planning and sensitivity to the wealth of resources that abound in the

natural environment can be capitalized upon with minimal expenditures of funds.

Assumption 2: Carefully examining roles and responsibilities, a staff can commit portions of their time to implementing a parent involvement program. If doing so ranks as priority area, arrangements can be made that free each staff member to devote short periods of time to the project. By reviewing all the adult resources available to the program—such as teachers, teacher aides, volunteer groups, parents and tutors—modifications can be made in scheduling and assigning tasks.

Assumption 3: Even extremely busy parents have to drop their children off in the morning and pick them up in the evening. Parents are most likely to be found at home in the evenings or on weekends. Time to make contact is therefore available; but the staff must know when, where and how!

Assumption 4: Most parents will not come knocking at your door to demand an education program. Many of them do not perceive themselves serving an important role as teachers of their own children, and they rarely have access to information suggesting what they can do. You can develop interest by planning as carefully for and with parents as you do in the case of children. The staff can capitalize on interests of the parents by asking them to participate in setting relevant goals. Once this is done, activities and materials can be designed to support attaining the goals. The key motivational strategies are: building on interest, providing relevant experiences, sequencing tasks to achieve a "match," and reinforcing appropriate behaviors by providing feedback to the participants.

61

STRATEGIES FOR IMPLEMENTATION

Let us look now at some how-to's. The following strategies are a compendium of procedures that have been used successfully in a number of preschool programs.

Contacting the Parent

To explore areas of concern and clarify major purposes of the parent-involvement program, you need to make initial contact with each parent. Through home visits or appointments at school in the early morning or evening, focus discussion on why the program is important and clarify goals, the amount of time you will ask parents to commit, what they will learn and gain, the potential effects on their children, and the program's system for recognizing parent accomplishments. Perhaps you can give each parent a printed handout that reviews all the topics covered and includes a form to return to school, indicating interest in participation.

Group Planning Meetings

Next, hold several group-planning meetings—at different times to accommodate varying work schedules—for all interested parents. Mail announcements or send them home with the children and follow up with telephone calls or personal contact inviting each parent to attend. Your agenda for the group-meeting should include time for introductions and informal conversation, sharing of concerns and discussion of possible goals and activities. Perhaps the staff can present a general overview of the program, show samples of materials that have been developed (based on topics identified in the initial phase), and demonstrate how parents could use them at home. If time permits, the parents can then break into small groups and role-play some of the ideas presented.

Fifteen Minutes a Day

Look around your school facility and find a spot close to the entrance where you can set up a filmstrip projector and a cassette tape recorder. Turn this area into a Parents' Corner, and let your parents know that every week new materials will be displayed. Encourage them to drop by in the morning or evening and take a few minutes to check out the ideas for the week. Begin with short slide-cassette presentations that deal with basic principles of child development, such as the importance of encouraging curiosity and exploration and of asking questions, talking to the child, reinforcing appropriate behavior, etc. Use pictures of children enrolled in your program and develop a simple script that states a principle, describes examples of related behavior, and gives tips for follow-up at home. Your sequence of presentation should include a clear statement of basic information, many concrete examples, and printed materials reviewing the main ideas presented and providing additional suggestions for parent-child interaction.

Weekly Tips

Building on the knowledge the parent acquires through the slide-tape presentations, develop activities—extending the information and encouraging parents to apply the basic principles. Prepare and distribute printed materials that describe a number of different activities, using materials commonly found in the home. Try to capitalize on routines and activities occurring naturally during the day, rather than insisting that a special time be set aside. Examples of these events could include dressing and undressing the child, bathing, making beds, dusting, dealing with meal-time, washing and ironing clothes, taking out the garbage or working in the yard. Language development, in particular, can be stimulated by focusing children's attention on an ordinary event, asking questions and encouraging them to label, describe, compare, contrast or predict what might happen.

Workshop Meetings

After two or three months have passed, hold a series of meetings with parents to review what has happened. These might be good times to present samples of progress charts based on goals for the parents and the children. Encourage the participants to individualize the charts by setting goals important to them. For example, one parent might want to work toward reinforcing positive behavior, rather than punishing negative behavior. Another might want to begin reading regularly to her child or to work toward encouraging independence. Although some parents might require follow-up, this activity is critical for individualizing the program to meet specific, relevant goals.

After the meetings, send printed materials home to review decisions and describe what was done. Highlight suggestions made by the parents as well as ideas for learning materials that can be used at home. If the parents want to participate, try to schedule a workshop for making inexpensive learning materials. Parents might also take the initiative to organize and conduct workshops on their own.

Simple Kits—A Lending Library

You can design simple kits using inexpensive materials that will help the parent teach basic skills and concepts. Putting poker chips through a slot in the top of a coffee can, pouring or spooning activities and stacking-and-alignment games all contribute to developing fine motor-coordination. Simple games that teach basic colors, shapes and sizes, or develop the concepts of matching, sorting and seriation can be made from scraps of

materials. Simple instructions should accompany each kit, describing ways it can be used and encouraging parents to find new, creative extensions.

A series of cassette-slide presentations modeling adult-child interaction skills could be developed around these kits. It is most important that parents see the joy and spontaneity that can occur when a child is involved in learning, rather than view the printed instructions as a stilted script. Tape different adult-models, including parents enrolled in the program, to illustrate a wide variety of teaching styles and interaction skills. Put the kits on display in your Parents' Corner and encourage the parents to check them out and use them.

Free Resource Materials

Every community is full of free resources. Survey what is available in your community. Don't forget grocery stores (boxes), carpet firms (rug samples), paint stores (color chips), lumberyards (scrap lumber) or fabric stores (texture samples). Collect as much as you can and make samples for display in your Parents' Corner—things parents can make. Include outdoor materials whenever possible to encourage large-muscle coordination and development. Again, get and share feedback from the parents who create new uses for basic materials.

Places To Go

Just as every community offers resources for free materials, also available are places of educational interest to children and parents. Another survey is in order, this time with camera in hand. Plan a display of places of interest to visit and include directions as well as any costs involved. In your Parents' Corner you might set up slide-cassette presentations describing what can be seen and particular points of interest. This kind of learning activity can be geared to the whole family, with tips for extending involvement included in the presentation. Accompanying printed materials might include directions, costs (if any), goals and follow-up activities for home. For example, if the family visits the zoo, encourage the parents to check out books at the local library on animals. The parent can teach his child to recognize various animals, describe and compare them. The child can be encouraged to recall all the animals he saw and then find the pictures in the book.

EVALUATING YOUR PROGRAM

How do you know whether or not all of the effort committed to the working-together program is worthwhile? You won't know unless you plan to evaluate the effects from the first day the idea is discussed. Your design does not have to be elaborate, but without careful planning it will be impossible to make decisions about continuing the effort or improving the quality of the program. Here are some basic questions to ask; in addition, you will of course want to develop specific questions of interest to your own group:

How many parents indicated initial interest?

How many parents attended group meetings or, if they missed the meetings, contacted a staff member individually?

How many printed handouts on activities and materials were picked up by parents?

How many parents offered comments (verbally or in writing) on using activity-ideas or kits?

How often did parents involved in the program contact or talk to the classroom teacher about their child's progress in the center or school?

How many parents filled in the progress charts and reviewed attainment of goals with staff?

What kinds of comments did the parents make about how they perceived themselves as teachers of their own children?

What differences were observed in the behavior of children whose parents were involved in the parent-program (trying new tasks, persisting, asking questions, expressing self freely, showing independence, self-starting, etc.)?

Finally, how many parents volunteer to continue active involvement in the program?

Regardless of the result of the evaluation, give formal recognition to all parents who committed time and participated in the program. One effective technique is to combine the recognition ceremonies with a social event, such as a coffee or community supper. Certificates of accomplishment might be awarded to the parents (and teachers!) who have worked toward and achieved goals. For those who wish to continue, this might prove a good time to develop cooperatively new goals for the coming year and to consider other strategies and activities. Acknowledge weaknesses, talk about all of the ideas that didn't work, and cooperatively review new approaches that will assist you in "working with parents on the run."

References

Bronfenbrenner, U. *A Report on Longitudinal Evaluations of Preschool Programs: Is Early Intervention Effective?* Vol. 2. DHEW Publication No. (OHD) 74-25.

Gilmer, B.; J. Miller; & S. Gray. *Intervention with Mothers and Young Children. Study of Intra-Family Effects.* Nashville, TN: DARCEE Demonstration & Research Center for Early Education, 1970.

Gordon, I. *A Home Learning Center Approach to Early Stimulation.* Gainesville, FL: Institute for Development of Human Resources, 1971 (Grant No. MH16037-02).

Karnes, M.; A. Hodgins, & J. Teska. "The Impact of At-Home Instruction by Mothers on Performance in the Ameliorative Preschool." In *Research and Development Program on Preschool Disadvantaged Children: Final Report,* M. B. Karnes. Washington, DC: U.S. Office of Education, 1969. Pp. 205-212.

Klaus, R., & S. Gray. *The Early Training Project for Disadvantaged Children: A Report After Five Years.* Monographs of the Society for Research in Child Development 33, 4, Serial #120 (1968).

Levenstein, P. "Cognitive Growth in Preschoolers Through Verbal Interaction with Mothers." *American Journal of Orthopsychiatry* 40 (1970): 426-32.